PAST DUE
How To Collect
Money

PAST DUE

How To Collect Money

NORMAN KING

PAST DUE: How To Collect Money

LIBRARY OF CONGRESS CATALOGING IN PUBLICATION DATA

King, Norman
Past due.

Includes index.
1. Collection of accounts. I. Title.
HG3752.5.A33 1983   658.8′8   82-21151
ISBN 0-87196-140-7

Printed in the United States of America

10 9 8 7 6 5 4 3 2 1

Designed by Giorgetta Bell McRee

CONTENTS

CHAPTER ONE

The Collections Crunch

Not too many years ago a familiar sign used to hang on back-bar mirrors and walls of soda fountains and drygoods stores:

**IN GOD WE TRUST
ALL OTHERS PAY CASH**

Anyone seeing such a sign today might well wonder what it meant. With credit cards and installment-plan buying, it's rare to pay cash for anything other than the most trivial purchases. Ironically, about the only cash a person really needs to carry is that special twenty dollars for the mugger, which can save one from having his throat slit!

In fact, the saws from another era concerning thrift make absolutely no sense today. Take "A penny saved is a penny earned." A penny saved at 5½ percent interest is simply not even a penny anymore when the yearly inflation rate runs at 6 or 8 percent. It is, in effect, a penny put gently to death. A penny *spent* is the only penny whose value has been actually received.

With deficit spending an almost institutionalized method of doing business in government, even Micawber's famous aphorism in *David Copperfield* no longer applies: "Annual income twenty pounds, annual expenditure nineteen six, result happiness. Annual income twenty pounds, annual expenditure twenty pounds eight and six, result misery."

In the 1980s, Micawber's second condition would actually be keeping up with inflation; he would simply take out a loan of eight and sixpence to make up the difference.

THE BEGINNINGS OF DEFICIT SPENDING

America—indeed the world—was operating on a cash-and-carry basis up through the Great Depression. Benjamin Franklin's observations on thrift were in everyone's mind; Micawber's advice made good sense. With national economies stagnated in the 1930s because of a lack of credit and a lack of cash flow, governments the world over introduced a new method of reviving their depressed economies: deficit spending.

At the close of World War II, prosperity, save for the 1946–50 recession, once again had returned to the economies of the West. It was then that the public took to living on credit as if it were the only possible way to go. In 1945, installment consumer debt stood at $2.5 billion—certainly not an inconsiderable sum. However, within one decade, that figure rose to $29 billion—more than ten times greater. In another decade, it reached $100 billion—and it has continued to spiral upward since.

The crowning irony of those years, for anyone who lived through the Great Depression, was the fact that credit had become *more* important than cash. Previously, to open a credit account at a department store, one had to prove that he had already borrowed money or had obtained credit elsewhere. Now all that was necessary was that he be able to keep his charge account paid up!

The importance of credit was lost on neither the business-person nor the merchant. "Buy now, pay later" became the slogan for the era of open credit. It was taken up by everyone.

THE INCREASE IN DISCRETIONARY INCOME

The prosperity of the 1950s was not based on inflation and paper profits. However, with the increase in family incomes, what was called *discretionary income*—money beyond that needed to provide basic subsistence—increased at an extraordinary rate. The economy was stimulated into an escalating situation that provided something for everyone.

With Vietnam, America found itself involved in a conflict that required no immediate personal sacrifice on the home front; a "Fight Now, Pay Later" mentality prevailed.

The early to mid-1960s was a time of unprecedented prosperity; a time when American youths could afford to "do their thing," drawing on income from home.

By the 1970s, credit was something that *everyone* had. Credit became a way of life, and it was a good life. Inflation was still proceeding at a relatively slow rate; nothing threatened the good life.

WHEN THE BILLS ALL CAME DUE

In the mid-1970s several factors occurred almost simultaneously. The United States withdrew from Vietnam, and the bills came due for the enormous war machine that the nation had fabricated. Internationally, the world's leading oil-exporting nations quadrupled prices, forcing the country to pay much more for what it had always gotten cheaply.

The policies of the Organization of Petroleum Exporting Countries, the dramatic decline of the industrial might of America, numerous bank failures (where there had been few since the Depression), the faltering of the stock market and sudden rising joblessness pointed the way to readjustment and reassessment.

But by that time, the American people were so used to the easy availability of credit and the habit of spending money that they did not heed the warnings. When the bills came due, they were ignored. Things would always get better; money would come in—so thought the average person.

However, prices were beginning to rise with unprecedented rapidity; inflation was suddenly an incubus on every American's back, causing untold misery immediately to those who had always lived on the fringes. Even those people who had always been "comfortable" in the past were made now to feel just a bit—and unexpectedly—uncomfortable.

The economy was not yet in deep trouble, but certain individuals were. They had based their spending philosophy on the government's. That is, if one can't pay one's bills, one simply spends, and then borrows to finance payment later. By now the borrowing was extended so far ahead, even for the government, that the future began to look a bit doubtful even to the most optimistic.

THE SQUEEZE ON THE CREDITOR

During the prosperous years, utilities such as electric and water companies had waited for their money fairly patiently when individual customers were unable to pay their bills. Usually the bills were paid, even if they were late. In the late 1970s, the picture began to change. Individuals found that when they missed payments, they began to get insistent dunning letters, and they were threatened with having their service cut off or the overdue bills turned over to professional collectors.

For many people receiving such treatment, it was the first time in their lives they had ever been reprimanded for slow payment. At first, most resented the implication that they were deadbeats. Many of them straightened up and began paying more attention to their small debts.

But not all.

With the feverish escalation of inflation in the late 1970s, even small bills became difficult to pay. People who were making good salaries had their water shut off, their power shut off and their telephones disconnected.

Many people let such bills slide and didn't pay them until absolutely necessary. Collections became more difficult for every type of businessperson. Many utilities and even department stores found it difficult to keep their books straight. Smaller suppliers to larger companies found that the companies did not pay up their debts as quickly as they once had. When the middle suppliers discovered their cash flow reduced, they too resorted to holding up payments for *their* supplies. Doctors and dentists found that many of their most trustworthy patients were not paying accounts with their usual speed.

Worse yet, by the late 1970s it was becoming almost fashionable to stall payments—or avoid paying legitimate debts entirely, a trend no doubt linked to the rising interest rates. The shift in the public's attitude toward paying bills can be seen in some of the book titles of the period:

- *A Lawyer Tells You How to Get Out of Debt . . . and Stay Out*
- *Strategies of the Harassed Bill Payer*
- *The Bill Collector and How to Cope with Him*
- *How to Get Your Creditor Off Your Back Without Losing Your Shirt*

And the all-time best-seller in the same vein: *Your Check Is in the Mail.*

The last, quite simply, was a personable and practical primer on the art of avoiding payment of bills for as long as possible.

People who had always paid their bills became slowpays, no-pays and then deadbeats.

HELP FOR THE SMALL BUSINESSPERSON

This book does not intend to pinpoint the cause of all this misery. But it does intend to give substantial help to the small

5

businessperson, the professional and the individual proprietor involved in trying to collect overdue bills.

Whatever its causes, the slow-payment syndrome of the 1980s is a national disgrace, perhaps an international disgrace. Credit, which was initially advanced to try to bring the economy out of the doldrums and get things moving again, became a tool for the unscrupulous and a weapon of self-destruction for the unwary.

Easy credit tempted the fly-by-night merchant to sell shoddy material, on the theory that once the sale was made, the bills could be collected, by force if necessary.

Easy credit also tempted the borderline consumer, who had some money but not really enough to buy that big bedroom set, to sign for merchandise on installment terms and then delay in paying the bills when the due date came.

The temptations on both sides helped produce the glut of bankruptcies, mergers, corporate takeovers and general malaise that is characteristic of the business world of the 1980s. Now, with inflation more or less under control, this credit malaise has caused millions of Americans to overspend, with no way to pay for the necessities—much less the luxuries!—to keep them alive.

Sympathy for the dunned consumer is at an all-time high. But what about the merchant, the small businessperson, the professional, the individual trying to do a job, who cannot keep in business when his accounts due are so difficult to collect? What recourse does he have? Moreover, what about honest consumers who have to pay higher prices to cover the bad debts of the deadbeats?

America is not England of the 1820s, when Charles Dickens's father was thrown into debtor's prison as punishment for his unpaid bills. Today, in America, there are so many laws and restrictions placed upon the businessperson or professional who cannot collect an honest debt—created at the insistence of well-meaning consumer advocates who unfortunately fail to see that the collector is not wholly the villain—that it is difficult to know how to move or where to turn to get money that is owed.

However, certain effective, time-tested procedures are available. And there are expediencies and alternatives to which the individual can turn for help to collect debts from dead-beats. To examine them is the purpose of this book. By studying *Past Due*, the small businessperson, the professional and the individual proprietor can learn proper procedures in the complex art of settling accounts with overdue debtors.

CHAPTER TWO

The How and Why of Credit

Before going into the problems of collecting unpaid bills, it is first necessary to find out what causes people to pile up debts. Even more than that, it is necessary to find out why some people never let debts lapse and why others habitually do.

In a cash-and-carry society, in which no person can take possession of any commodity—especially durable goods—without exchanging money for it, there is no need to study collection techniques. Obviously, there are no unpaid bills. Deadbeats are a product—some would say the scourge—of a society that does its business mostly on credit.

WHAT IS CREDIT?

Before defining methods used to determine a person's "credit risk"—that is, the probable swiftness or slowness of eventual payment—it is a good idea to know exactly what credit is.

We live today in a society based fundamentally on credit;

many of our current economic problems stem from its abuse. Yet even Webster is not any too clear on a definition. The closest any one of the different explanations comes in the dictionary is: "financial or commercial trustworthiness." Basically, credit means, for the average person, his or her ability to obtain goods or services in exchange for a promise to pay for them later on.

A man or woman goes into a store to purchase goods. He or she has a checkbook and a driver's license. After comparing the identification on the driver's license with the check, the proprietor okays the purchase and accepts the check in payment. At one time, a customer would have had to pay for the purchase with cash. Today, most anyone who looks respectable, has a checkbook and carries a valid driver's license can purchase goods in a store simply by appearing trustworthy and projecting the image of a solid citizen.

And so, in a general way, the meaning of "credit" is equated with "trustworthiness." A prospective consumer who *looks* trustworthy becomes a good credit risk. This type of credit is called *consumer credit*, for obvious reasons. There are various kinds of consumer credit, including retail charge-account credit, installment-sales credit and the service account.

THE RETAIL CHARGE ACCOUNT

The *retail charge account* is set up to enable the customer to purchase goods at a department store or small shop on a regular basis. To open such a charge account, the consumer fills out a form requesting that a charge account be opened in his or her name. There are several different kinds of charge accounts, but the most common type is the account which sends out a monthly statement to inform each customer of the number of purchases made during that period and the total amount owed for these purchases.

The consumer pays the monthly bill regularly during the year. The material purchased is never paid for in cash at the point of sale, but is handed over "on credit," that is, on the

9

supposition by the seller that the bill for the purchase will be paid at the end of the billing period.

A charge account may also offer various ways to pay up large bills, usually on an installment basis. A large purchase can thus be paid up in several installments, say, in three months rather than in just one month. Interest may be charged for this type of service; often it is not.

To establish the consumer charge account, the customer refers the credit manager of the store to other charge accounts, to the bank where the customer has an account or to other credit managers who will vouch for him or her. If the consumer has a bad credit record, he becomes a bad credit risk; the store thinks twice before opening the account.

THE SERVICE ACCOUNT

A slightly different type of account is the *service account,* in which the consumer does not open a charge account to purchase durable goods, but rather to obtain a service of some kind or other, usually relating to an appliance or piece of machinery. The typical consumer-professional relationship is a service account—for example, the patient-doctor or client-lawyer relationship—based on mutual trust. The person offering the service must determine in advance if the client to be serviced is trustworthy and able to pay for his service.

In a typical relationship with a professional—a lawyer, doctor, dentist or accountant—billing is usually done on an individual basis, with each bill referring to a specific visit or service.

There are also service accounts for customers available with artisans, mechanics and other craftspersons. Typically, a service contract on a furnace is issued on the basis of a yearly fee, with the serviceperson required to handle repairs and adjustments during the period of the contract. This type of contract is based on credit, too. As such, the consumer's credit rating must be investigated before the contract is drawn up.

Such a service contract is usually billed on a yearly basis or in installments during the year. In a way it resembles a "retaining fee" for the services of the craftsperson, assuring him or her in advance a particular fee for a particular job.

BUSINESS OR MERCANTILE CREDIT

There is another type of credit called *business credit*, also known as *mercantile credit*. This type of credit is advanced by a supplier to a firm purchasing the products or services of an individual or a small company. For example, the individual or firm that supplies a certain type of valve to a manufacturer of mechanical equipment sells the valves to the manufacturer on a promise of payment within a specified billing period.

The valve fabricator, having predetermined that the manufacturer will pay for the goods, has extended credit to the manufacturer by the shipment of the merchandise.

In general, these are the kinds of credit that I will discuss in this book. There are other types—public credit, which deals with federal bonds, notes, certificates, bills and currency; state credit, which deals with bonds and notes; and municipal credit, which deals with bonds, notes and certificates—but they have little to do with the kind of credit that the average consumer is acquainted with and the type of credit that can be a source of slow-payment or nonpayment of personal debts.

CONSUMER CREDIT VERSUS BUSINESS CREDIT

Consumer credit is quite different from business credit. It is a type of credit granted to a consumer to expedite the process of the consumption of goods. From the consumer's point of view, credit is the power to obtain goods and services, the ability to borrow money for the purpose of consumption with the promise to pay at a future date.

Broadly speaking, consumer credit includes all the types of credit extensions known for personal use granted by manufacturers, producers, retailers, professionals, service organizations or by various types of financial institutions. (Even mortgage loans are considered credit; they are not covered in this book because the creditor is usually a bank.)

Consumer credit is open-book credit, installment-sales credit and credit arising out of the borrowing of cash by consumers to pay for goods or services.

THE PURPOSE OF CREDIT

In the long run, there is only one good reason for credit at all—to make a profit:

- To the merchant who sells durable goods, it helps effect an increased volume of sales and a profitable business income.
- To the banker, it means a worthwhile return on investment and compensation for an efficient mode of operation.

To the consumer, it is not quite so obvious. The individual using credit is motivated by a complicated combination of desires and drives. They are usually three in number: convenience, upward mobility and necessity.

CONVENIENCE

Convenience is obviously the most important and recognizable stimulation for the consumer to use credit. Millions of buyers use credit every year because they find it a convenient way in which to obtain goods and services. The buyer can place an order by telephone; the consumer can purchase goods at a large store simply by invoking a charge account; more than one member of a family can purchase goods on a single account without the need to carry large sums of cash about.

Payment for these purchases is easily made by a periodic settling of accounts. The credit system helps the consumer budget his money directly at the source. The bill payer can then control expenses easily and readily at all times.

The theory makes sense. It is the inability to keep the process running smoothly that leads to problems like overdue collections and unpaid accounts.

UPWARD MOBILITY

Upward mobility is the next most obvious reason for the use of credit. Credit-card purchasing, installment buying and charge-account spending is a quick and easy means of improving the standard of living. The acquisition of television sets, video games, automobiles, home appliances and furniture makes life somewhat easier to bear, and helps to improve one's perceived position in the world.

Credit can even help one to borrow money to finance a vacation, to make home repairs or improvements or to send a child to college. All that is necessary is the ability to pay for these loans when they come due.

NECESSITY

Necessity is the most viable reason for the establishment of credit. Certain types of lifestyle demand ready credit to keep going even on a bare-subsistence level. To the farmer, credit to get through to the next year is an absolute must. Without some kind of credit, no farmer would survive.

Industrial workers sometimes run into cycles of recession or unemployment in which credit is the only thing that keeps the family in food and clothing.

Individuals can incur emergencies like accidents, sickness, or death or run into bouts of illness that require hospitalization, special medical care and other problems. Credit can help such people through the bad periods when there is not enough money at hand to pay the bills.

THE ABUSE OF CREDIT

It is obvious that credit is a part of the fabric that holds our society together. It is the *abuse* of credit that concerns the small businessperson, the professional and the individual proprietor caught in today's collections squeeze.

Because credit is now available to almost anyone who wants it, the credit granter must be more cautious in deciding whether or not to extend it to individuals or companies. The creditor must be more alert in spotting the potential nonpayer *in advance*. The process of collecting money granted on credit actually begins before the first sale of a product or the first proffer of a service. It begins with the original agreement between creditor and debtor.

Making the right credit decision at the *beginning* of the contract is the *key* element in collections.

It is the subject of the following chapter, and, in fact, underlines all the discussions in the chapters that follow.

CHAPTER THREE
Determining Credit Risks

A basic problem of collecting money on overdue bills is simply this: not all debtors are alike. Nor, for that matter, are all debts alike. Just as some debtors are flush with money and anxious to pay bills quickly so as to move on to other things, so are many strapped for funds and forced to put off paying their accounts as long as possible. Just as some debts are small and easy to pay, so others are cumbersome and difficult to pay off on a tight schedule.

Each individual situation is special. In order to make decisions regarding action on unpaid bills clearcut and accurate, it is common practice to grade payers of bills into several distinct classifications. These categories help the creditor to determine the speed, frequency and intensity with which reminders of payment should be made.

In order to categorize all potential debtors properly, an analysis of each should be made long before the first bill comes due. In fact, the most important decision the creditor can make is the original decision to grant credit. This decision must be accurate. An incorrect analysis can mean that the creditor may be involved in a slow-pay account or an account that will force the use of an attorney or a collection agency. It can even mean the involvement in bankruptcy, from which only partial payment may be recovered, or none at all.

There are six criteria for the granting of credit. These criteria—called the Six Cs—are the staples of the credit and collection business. They are easily remembered:

- Capacity
- Capability
- Character
- Circumstances
- Collateral
- Coverage.

Of these six, the first three pertain to the accurate analysis of the individual to whom the credit is to be extended. The second three refer to ancillary concerns in each case covered.

A more careful look at the Six Cs will provide some enlightenment on their importance.

THE SIX Cs

CAPACITY—THE ABILITY TO PAY THE BILLS

Capacity is sometimes referred to as *capital*, because the capacity of any company or individual to pay bills is based on the amount of capital invested in the company or in the possession of the individual. For the small businessperson or the individual engaged in providing a service or goods for a large company, there are many ways to check out the financial background of the buying firm. Dun & Bradstreet has provided credit ratings for many years, with profiles on thousands of companies.

For an individual for whom a professional or another individual provides service or goods, it is not quite so easy to determine true worth. The most logical way to find out whether or not a potential debtor will pay off or not is to look for other people who have been involved with the person in question and ask if there have been prior problems with collections.

In exploring capacity, the main thrust of the investigation is on the liquid assets of the company or person, not on the *appearance* of solvency. As many professionals and individual service personnel know, the image of affluence and prosperity can be a most misleading and tricky phenomenon. The con man will always be with us.

CAPABILITY—THE SKILL AND EXPERIENCE

Capability refers to a more intangible quality than capital. An individual or company with little capital may have tremendous potential for making a profitable income. At the same time, an individual or company with proper capital but with inferior capability may soon squander any advantage and wind up bankrupt.

Credit ratings provided by professional sources do not always accurately reflect true capability in the reports provided. Or, if they do, these judgments are sometimes far from objective and accurate. For the potential creditor, the bottom line on capability is usually reflected in the practical aspects of the firm of the individual's business. The successful client who had proved himself over the years is the one who has provided a good estimate of his capability in a practical and no-nonsense manner.

To the successful and prosperous company or individual go the highest marks in this difficult-to-judge quality.

CHARACTER—TRUST AND HONESTY

Even less tangible than capability is character. Trying to "read" a person's character can be impossibly difficult. The same is true of any small company or individual engaged in business. The problem in determining character in business is not the same as determining whether or not a man or firm is

17

honest or dishonest, good or evil, charismatic or hateful—it goes a good deal deeper than that.

Honesty and trust are primary considerations. However, the company and the individual's business dealings are really more to the point, not the individual's image or personality. The determination here involves the business enterprise itself— and its *character.*

First of all, is the business legitimate? Does it involve itself in dishonest endeavors? Can the principals be trusted? What is the company's history? Has it been involved in constant bickering and a long string of lawsuits? Does it have a history of slow payment?

Determination of a company's character has the same pitfalls as determination of a person's character. However, it is a most important consideration in trying to analyze a company's or individual proprietor's potential to pay off debts.

One of the best ways to find out about a potential client's character is through informal talks with people who are close to the company and who have worked for it.

CIRCUMSTANCES—FACTORS BEYOND IMMEDIATE CONTROL

The Fourth C has nothing whatsoever to do with the company of the individual under credit investigation. Life itself is made up of circumstances: bad weather, good weather; drought, sickness and disease; flood, fire, famine and earthquake; recession, inflation, prosperity.

Although circumstances beyond the control of either principal in a credit relationship have nothing to do with the company or individual, they must always be taken into account as a relevant variable that may have bearing on any situation to come.

In other words, the product or service involved may suddenly decline in value. There may be no more need for certain goods; today the horseshoe is used in a game, not to shoe horses by the millions. Hula hoops came and went in what seemed like days. A flood or fire may damage a company's plant beyond hope of recovery. A war may wipe out a certain type of commodity or service.

There is no way to predict circumstances. Fate is a variable factor that must be allowed for; however, in some cases, an intelligent investigation of the situation may suggest certain eventualities. If the creditor is prepared, he will have covered himself before the catastrophe occurs.

COLLATERAL—TANGIBLE GUARANTEES OF PAYMENT

Collateral is almost a "last resource" in a creditor's analysis. To determine collateral is to look at the worst possible aspect of the relationship between creditor and debtor. Nevertheless, it is always a possibility that the worst will happen and disaster will occur.

Collateral means security, the amount of a firm's business that is held as security by another. It also means the amount of a firm's business that can be immediately turned into cash in order to pay off debts.

A creditor should determine if his potential buyer can offer a tangible guarantee—in the form of collateral—that the bills for the service or goods received will be paid.

COVERAGE—INSURANCE AND ASSURANCE

Circumstances in the form of disasters occur frequently enough in any business transaction to force the creditor to recognize the fact. Insurance covering instances of fire, explosion, flood, earthquake and even the death of the company owner is a different consideration from recognition of fate and "circumstances." Insurance coverage is a tangible thing; consideration of the possibility of recession or depression is intangible. A creditor should find out if the potential buyer has sufficient insurance to protect the property and the company against the kinds of disasters that can ruin an enterprise.

In other words, there are proper channels for compensating the effects of natural disasters. Coverage by insurance assures the creditor of eventual recovery of money. However, in the case of financial reversals and business fluctuations, no such insurance is available. The only way to defend against them is to determine whether or not such eventualities are likely in the near future, and decide accordingly.

DETERMINING AMOUNT OF CREDIT

In addition to Six Cs, a creditor must also determine how much credit he can extend in relation to the worth of the company or individual.

If a shipment of goods involves $50,000, the creditor certainly does not want to risk the extension of credit in that amount if he discovers that the firm to which he is shipping has only $5000 in the bank and a net worth of $25,000.

Nor would a creditor supplying services or goods worth $5000 extend credit to an individual who has a net worth of only $3000.

Creditors use a yardstick to determine the amount of shipment that is worth the risk. It involves determining the firm's net worth first and then measuring that against the size of the shipment. The ratio is ten to one, net worth to credit.

For example, if the firm to be granted the credit has a net worth of $5000, it is considered safe—if all other factors are equal (the Six Cs, for example)—to ship $500 worth of goods or perform $500 worth of service.

However, in instances where the other factors under consideration—the Six Cs, for example—are all uniformly good, the ten-to-one factor can be stretched a bit, in favor of the potential debtor.

THE REST OF THE STORY

Of course, determining credit risk is only one half of the story. What happens later on—when Firm A or Individual A fails to pay bills on time, or when Firm A and Individual A pays up on time—helps to classify each debtor in the creditor's mind. It also determines future handling of each account.

For example, the individual or company failing to pay bills on time should be treated with more speed and firmness than an individual or company never before in arrears.

In order to categorize each potential debtor, the credit should divide credit customers into three main classes: good risks, fair risks and poor risks.

THE GOOD RISK

The customer who has a high rating in regard to his financial ability to pay and who has an excellent business character, is a good-pay customer with a high credit limit. When he cannot pay on time (for whatever reason), he usually makes satisfactory arrangements to somehow pay the bill.

This is the customer who should be treated with the greatest respect and courtesy—especially in the case of a delinquency over which he has no control. The good risk should only be reminded of the payment of an overdue bill. Most customers who are good risks are sensitive; the creditor must treat them mildly, leniently and courteously. Any other treatment may cause them to be offended and withdraw their patronage.

In dealing with a good risk, the creditor should not resort to drastic measures. The time between the various steps in the collection schedule should be stretched out as far as possible.

THE FAIR RISK

In the second category comes the customer who has a high rating but whose ability to pay is not quite so good as the good risk's. He may be careless, or he may run a company that is not quite as successful as its competitors. That is, his capability, his character and his capacity to pay may combine to force him into a situation where his cash flow is a problem.

He is not a customer who is *deliberately* trying to hang onto his money and not meet his obligations. He is simply caught in unfortunate circumstances, unable to keep up with his payments. He needs to be handled discreetly, but still with more firmness than the good risk who becomes involved in a temporary setback.

The fair risk is honest, has a good basic character and has the ability to succeed, but is burdened by business reversals and other considerations. However, he does not want to be pressured and embarrassed by quick threats of court suits and collection agencies. He should be handled gingerly.

With the proper treatment and handling, the fair risk can become a good risk. However, with too much pressure and aggravation, the fair risk can soon fall back into the third category, the poor risk, and be lost to the creditor.

Of the three categories, his handling is the most difficult and subtle.

THE POOR RISK

The chronic deadbeat is the customer who simply has never had the ability to pay on time and has the reputation of never meeting his obligations with even fair promptitude. His credit line should be kept low and strictly overseen.

Some deadbeats are actually unable to pay on time; they are psychologically incapable of doing so. Many of these deadbeats have grown up in an economy in which paying bills is not the most important factor in business. They think credit means not paying.

Others in this category simply cannot pay their debts on time. There is always something that goes wrong with the business, or there are contingencies that have not been thought out or provided for ahead of time. Poor management, incompetence, poor capacity—all these relevant variables help create a bad-risk debtor.

These bad risks must be kept on a tight leash. If kept there, within reason, most of their payments may be expected within a reasonable time—but never on the dot at due date.

Handling the honest non-deadbeat bad risk requires greater delicacy than handling the true deadbeat. Although the letters of reminder and the letters of discussion should be spaced out with much smaller intervals than with the fair risk, the poor risk should be reminded that he must come up with the money as soon as possible. Sympathy, help and even extensions should be granted the honest non-deadbeat. In this category, the creditor must show patience and understanding.

For the true deadbeat, only quick reminders and threats of collection agencies or attorneys will help. No sympathy should be shown to individuals who have earned a reputation as chronic bad-pay customers. Usually the deadbeat has such a thick skin that he simply cannot be insulted or prompted to take his business elsewhere.

PSYCHOLOGICAL CRITERIA FOR ANALYZING DEBTORS

In addition to categorizing each customer as to his credit risk, the creditor should also analyze his psychological profile. Each individual, as well as each firm, is unique. Usually the company takes its character from its president, particularly true of a small business firm, and obviously true for the professional and the individual proprietor.

Some creditors divide slow-paying customers into eight basic psychological types. If a customer is a combination of several of these basic types, the creditor should study the suggestions for handling each and exercise creative judgment in merging them into a unified working approach.

1. Nice but negligent businessperson
2. Honest but confused businessperson
3. Person too big for small debts
4. Seasonal delinquent
5. Disaster victim
6. Chronically slow-pay
7. Individual who is broke but unbowed
8. True deadbeat

NICE BUT NEGLIGENT

In the first category is the individual who is fundamentally and irremediably a procrastinator. He has the *mañana* syndrome; nothing can snap him out of it. He is late for appointments, he is late for casual get-togethers. He simply won't adhere to rules of any kind involving time, but must be reminded when any due date comes around.

This type of personality needs a wary, almost hands-off treatment—although when a reminder, etc. is actually sent, he must be handled with extreme firmness. Usually the procrastinator simply does not understand all the fuss about lateness. For that reason, he demands cautious and careful treatment—even more than the person who *knows* he's late and simply doesn't care.

HONEST BUT CONFUSED

In the second category is the person who should never be involved in business at all. However, given the society in which we live, he has to do something. It is the creditor's unlucky break to have to do business with him.

Whether his helplessness or confusion is due to actual fogginess of intellect or to profound self-indulgence and years of bumbling is beside the point. He must be helped, with reasonableness and kindness. Like the nice but negligent individual, the honest but confused businessperson must be handled with kid gloves. He is the first to take offense at any suggestion that he is incompetent. Usually, with some guidance, he manages to pay the bills and keep the accounts open.

Amazingly enough, the honest but confused person quite frequently makes a great deal of money and is looked up to as a model businessperson—by anyone who does not have to collect money from him!

Obviously, he must be handled with tact.

TOO BIG FOR SMALL DEBTS

Although at first glance the businessperson who thinks of small debts as beneath his consideration might seem to be a deadbeat covering up his nonpayment of bills, he is actually able to pay but does not want to settle for small amounts. Quite sincere in his inability to see the need to pay up these negligent amounts immediately, he believes in lumping big amounts together and paying them up later on.

It is not procrastination that motivates him. It is simply the fact that he wants to pay his debts in big chunks and not waste time on "nickel and dime stuff." He usually pays up a small amount with the next big bill. Handling him is a problem. He usually takes umbrage at being reminded about the small long-overdue debt.

THE SEASONAL DELINQUENT

Some businesses only thrive during periods in which certain kinds of activity flourish. When the cash flow slows down and such a customer is not making enough sales, he often simply refuses to pay. Instead of setting some money aside to tide him over the dry days, he stops paying until the cash flow starts up again.

This kind of thinking drives many creditors up the wall. How to handle the slow seasonal payer is a question that has never been properly answered. To cut him off is ridiculous; when business picks up in the rush season, he pays his bills on time. The creditor must be able to differentiate the seasonal delinquent from the deadbeat who is *pretending* to be a seasonal delinquent.

THE DISASTER VICTIM

Floods, fires, earthquakes, wars, strikes, civil strife and disease occur randomly. The debtor who becomes victim to natural disaster is a very special case. Provisions are usually made—through insurance, through government aid, through banking help—to get him back on his feet after a ruinous event.

Acts of God cannot be controlled, even by the most astute businessperson. The creditor should extend every courtesy to the victim of disaster, and wait until it is possible for him to pay up his debts.

THE CHRONICALLY SLOW-PAY

Like the nice but negligent and the honest but confused debtor, the chronically slow-pay is overdue because of a constitutional inability to rush. Something in this individual's personality prevents him from seeing the necessity to pay up a bill on time. It is not a simple case of procrastination; it is a constitutional failure to keep moving in the swim with everyone else.

A first cousin to the chronically slow is an alternate type: the undercapitalized businessperson. He's a smart individual who knows his business, but he has never really had enough money to run his shop efficiently. For one reason or another, he is so undercapitailzed that he cannot pay his bills on time; he has to make up his capital deficit by taking out an interest-free loan from you—his creditor—by stretching out his payments as long as you'll let him.

For both these personality types, the creditor must exercise a great deal of care and patience in order not to alienate and lose them forever.

BROKE BUT UNBOWED

Sometimes business conditions are such that even a good businessperson is unable to pay his bills. In this event, the creditor must make some concessions in order to permit the debtor to continue in business and pay up his debts as soon as he can.

Because a number of skillful operators can make it *seem* as though there is no money to use, the creditor must be very sure of the debtor temporarily unable to pay what he owes. He must handle the situation circumspectly, trying to give the debtor all the help possible while making the debtor aware of the seriousness of the situation and concerned with payment as soon as possible.

THE TRUE DEADBEAT

Luckily there are not many true deadbeats in business—but there are enough to give even the most cautious creditor nightmares from time to time. The deadbeat actually believes in exercising every kind of deceptive practice possible in order not to pay off his debts.

The problem with the true deadbeat is that he is usually a man of many disguises. He can be acting as the negligent but nice, the honest but confused, even the disaster victim, without ever letting his true colors show.

Once the creditor establishes that the deadbeat has no intention of paying one red cent unless forced, he can then change his tactics and apply the pressure necessary—including all kinds of threats—to get the money. Once the money is obtained, the creditor then must break off all relations with the deadbeat, and try to warn anyone who will listen about the true nature of the person unmasked.

PROFILING THE DEBTOR

Once the person seeking credit has been properly pigeonholed through analysis of the Six Cs, determination of credit risk and psychological typing, he can be profiled by the creditor according to probable behavior.

Handling the debtor even after proper analysis can be a delicate business; the creditor must maintain complete records on all debtors at all times. The character and personality—and the behavior pattern—of the debtor may change over the years.

Records can also correct a faulty primary analysis and recategorize a debtor more accurately. Such movements will be due to his reaction to the steps the creditor takes in dealing with him through the collection process.

SPREADING THE WORD ABOUT DEADBEATS

Although some individuals today tend to distrust personnel records and profiles kept by organizations—claiming that such records are harbingers of a police-state mentality—such profiles are important to the person trying to determine someone's credit-worthiness. Care should be taken to check the accuracy of all data that goes into such files and to guarantee security for any private and confidential information involved.

For the credit manager of a small- or medium-sized company, not only his own records are important, but also the records of other credit managers of other companies. Most credit managers eventually become aware of poor risks, but it is a difficult and onerous process.

One good way to catch up on information about poor risks is for a credit manager to join a local or industry association of credit managers. At local meetings, he can then exchange information with other credit managers on specific deadbeats or other operators who tend to avoid paying up their accounts.

One national association that has eighty-odd local groups is the National Association of Credit Management (NACM), 475 Park Avenue South, New York, NY 10016. The association conducts workshops involving credit assessment, and also maintains a collection and adjustment service.

Other such associations exist. Credit managers can always find them in the yellow pages. These associations are a good place to exchange shop talk on the ups and downs of the credit business.

CHAPTER FOUR

The Successful Collection System

There's an old saw familiar to merchants everywhere since the beginning of credit: YOU MADE YOUR SALE—OR DID YOU?

In other words, there's no sale until the goods are paid for.

However, if the credit analysis has been accurate, and if all credit risks have been taken into consideration, most customers will pay their invoices on time—some a little slowly, a few even more slowly, but most of them will pay reasonably close to the due date.

For this reason, it is seldom necessary for the average small businessperson, professional or individual proprietor to have to place an account with a professional collector. Even a chronic slow-pay does not want to ruin his reputation by failing to settle eventually.

And yet it *is* the slow-pay individual who needs special handling. It is for that chronic procrastinator that a fool-proof, workable collection system has been devised.

THE HIGH COST OF SLOW PAYMENT

Most debtors have no conception of the problems aroused by tardy payment of bills, nor do many creditors. Yet every thirty days that a payment is delayed means less money in the bank for the creditor.

Money in the bank is necessary to pay bills and maintain overhead for any business. Without money, no firm can continue for long. That means that cash must be borrowed to make expenses and keep the business going.

With the current rates of interest so high, the cost of borrowing money is prohibitive. For example, if a creditor needs $1000 to maintain overhead, he pays $8.33 at 10 percent interest for one month only. For two months, the cost is $16.77; for three months, $25; and so on. At 11 percent interest, $1000 for one month costs $9.17—$110 for a year!

On the other hand, if the amount in arrears is $9000, borrowing that amount for one month costs $75 at 10 percent interest; $82.50 at 11 percent; and $115.50 at 15 percent. For one year, $9000 costs $1350 at the last amount!

This cost comes right off the top of all income; it cuts into profits; it may wipe out some businesses! It is simple enough to determine the *amount* of such a cost. Simply multiply the amount of the loan and the rate of interest in percentage, and divide by 12 months for the cost per month.

CUTTING INTO THE NET PROFIT

Looking at this problem in another way, suppose that the net profit on a sale of $1000 is 10 percent. By borrowing that $1000 to cover bills left unpaid, the net profit of $100 would be cut by $8.33 to $91.67. If the profit is only 2 percent on a $1000 sale, the cost of borrowing $1000 for one month would cut the profit of $20 to $11.67; by the time that particular bill remains unpaid for three months, the firm will *lose* $5 on the transaction! (One thousand dollars at 10 percent costs $25 for three months; $20 − $25 = −$5.)

Even if the firm does not actually need to borrow money, but can make up needed payments out of a cash balance, the reduction in profit still applies. The $1000, if received, could have been invested in short-term securities to build up emergency funds for other needs.

Cutting into profit is one side of the problem of unpaid bills. Looked at from another angle, the problem becomes even more troublesome. For an actual loss of $25, a firm operating at a net profit of 10 percent would have to make an additional sale of $250 to balance out the lost $25. Operating at a 2 percent net profit, the same firm would have to make a sale of $1250 to balance out a loss of $25. A loss of $1000 at 2 percent net profit would need additional sales of $50,000 to balance out.

DETERMINING THE EFFICIENCY OF A COLLECTION SYSTEM

It sometimes pays a company or individual to check out how well collections are doing over a certain period of time. One way is to divide the *total credit sales* for one month by the *total amount of accounts receivable,* and multiply the result by 30 days. The answer is the average collection period of the bills.

To obtain an ideal average collection, a firm can ascertain in advance how many days it should take for the average bill to be paid. Then divide the total amount of accounts receivable by the total credit sales for the month, and multiply by 30 days.

For the average collection period of the bills:
Suppose the total credit sales for one month is $1000, and the total amount of accounts receivable $900. One thousand dollars divided by $900 is 1.1; 1.1 multiplied by 30 is 33. The average collection period is 33 days.

For an optimum average collection period:
Suppose the figures are the same as above. Nine hundred

31

dollars divided by $1000 is 0.9; 0.9 multiplied by 30 is 27. The average optimum collection period is 27 days.

Collection methods and policies used by different types of businesses will differ, especially in regard to leniency or strictness. There are three specific elements involved in any collection system: promptness, regularity and systematization of effort.

THE COLLECTION SYSTEM

PROMPTNESS OF COLLECTION

Promptness is crucial. Without prompt payment of bills, the loss of revenue can cause extreme problems of indebtedness and force a firm to borrow money, as I've already explained. The success of any business venture depends on prompt payment of bills in order to keep money coming in, to keep collection costs and losses low and to preserve a reasonable standard of efficiency.

Promptness varies from one company to another. For example, a collection effort begun in thirty to sixty days may be considered prompt for a very good customer; on the other hand, five to fifteen days may be the maximum amount of time allowed to a customer prone to default.

It is also mandatory to try to collect installment bills more promptly than regular charge-account bills. Small businesses that operate in the merchandising area begin collection routines sooner than in other types of enterprise.

Promptness not only brings in money more quickly, but it exerts psychological control over the customer. It helps clear up any doubts the debtor may have about the seriousness of the bill-collecting procedure.

Also, by clearing up bills quickly, the creditor creates a situation in which the customer is induced to come back to buy more. By continuing in debt, a customer may shy away from buying more, or may turn elsewhere to purchase goods.

REGULARITY OF COLLECTION

Promptness and regularity are inseparable. A quick first reminder, not followed up immediately in the allotted time with a second reminder, becomes meaningless. The debtor tends to forget a lone reminder. No customer minds being jogged every so often, particularly if the reminder is regular, prompt and courteous.

A small firm that does not pay businesslike attention to the collection of its accounts, an individual who is too timid to remind a debtor of the money owed, any company that allows its accounts to slide further and further into debt, loses the respect of all its customers.

Indeed, constant reminders help keep some debtors in a more sound and healthy financial condition than could be expected without them.

SYSTEMATIZATION OF COLLECTION EFFORT

The successful maintenance of a collection system depends on the way in which the plan is originally drawn up. The system must be a logical, preplanned program, providing the same treatment for all comparable cases, and yet be able to deal with many different types of collection needs.

The principal aim is to allow the creditor to consider each delinquent account as an individual matter. For the average small business, there are usually not enough slow-paying customers to create a problem. Each account can be handled individually. However, a proper routine must be established for accomplishing the desired results.

The system should be developed so that a regular method of procedure can be used, beginning each individual collection effort with a reminder, and increasing pressure gradually until payment is received or until another method—a collection agency, an attorney or a visit to the small claims court—needs to be employed.

Psychologically, the creditor should try to intensify the impression made on the debtor by each step of the system, until it is strong enough to move the debtor to action.

At the same time, the system must be flexible enough to allow for differences in individual personality, financial condition and value of future patronage. No system should be so rigid that it becomes a mechanical, inhuman process.

The ideal system should be constructed in such a way that the creditor can use specialized and nonroutine methods if the collection effort necessitates a response not covered by the mechanics of the system.

HOW TO DETECT OVERDUE BILLS

Not every unpaid bill presents a collection problem. The payment of a bill during the credit period is not in any way considered a *collection* in the sense the word is used in this book—referring to an overdue, or delinquent, bill.

Collection refers specifically to the preplanned series of efforts used to achieve final payment after a debt has become past due. The primary consideration in collection strategy is to set up a system that keeps strict records of all bills past due—on a day-to-day basis. This strategy involves keeping clear, accurate records. The detection of an overdue bill becomes a simple step in the process of bookkeeping.

A number of practices have been devised to enable the creditor to initiate collection proceedings immediately on exposure of an overdue account. They include various techniques of providing instant recognition of nonpayment. These systems consist of records, files and policies and are known as collection-follow-up techniques.

Four of the most commonly used follow-up methods are the:

- Ledger system
- Card-tickler system
- Duplicate-invoice system
- Computerized system

The fourth of these will be covered in the next chapter. In principle, however, the computerized system is really nothing more than an automated or semi-automated variation on one or more of the three basic manual systems.

THE LEDGER SYSTEM

For the small businessperson and the individual proprietor, the simplest and most commonly used method of instituting collection is the ledger system. Very simply, the system is concentrated in the creditor's ledger records, that is, in the day-to-day bookkeeping files. The individual proprietor simply inspects the ledger at frequent intervals to determine which accounts are past due.

He then makes note of the nonpayment of the account on the ledger opposite the charge. With each succeeding step taken in the collection procedure, he adds further notation on the ledger until the bill is either paid up or disposed of in some other fashion.

This system is the least complicated of all collection systems and works admirably for the small businessperson, the professional or the individual proprietor. It also affords the creditor the opportunity—enforced by the collection procedure—of keeping an eye on the books to see how all accounts payable are faring.

Its advantage is its simplicity. No further records need be kept. All the notations and necessary remarks are kept in the business ledger where they can always be referred to. There is no need to sort out a multitude of papers or forms each day to check the progress of the collection effort.

However, there are disadvantages as well as advantages to the system. The most serious disadvantage is that it becomes a chore that may be postponed because more important tasks must be completed. When the collection system becomes irregular and haphazard, the entire collection plan falls apart.

Irregularity tends to make the effort of searching out delinquent accounts a secondary consideration, something to be done after everything else is completed. This in turn relegates the chore psychologically to lower priority, possibly causing the oversight of a large account until weeks have gone by.

Not only does the creditor sometimes forget overdue bills, but the careless debtor forgets them as well. Only strict adherence to a regular schedule of checking—say, every three working days, or every five working days—makes such a system viable.

For a business with a larger number of accounts, such a plan becomes unworkable. It is much too difficult to periodically sort through a large number of figures to find the few that require collection efforts. The search can interrupt the main work of the bookkeeper or bookkeeping department.

However, for the small business, for the professional and for the individual proprietor with a limited number of accounts, the ledger plan is the most viable and successful for searching out and targetting overdue bills.

THE CARD-TICKLER SYSTEM

For a small business or a professional who has a large number of customers, clients or suppliers, the card-tickler system provides a more practical and effective way of dealing with delinquencies.

It consists of a special file into which a card for each delinquent account is inserted according to the date of delinquency. The card contains the amount of the bill, the terms, the due date of the past-due amount and any collection actions taken so far, together with the dates.

Such a file is divided into thirty-one compartments, one for each day of the month. Each card is placed in the proper slot when the next step in the planned schedule takes place.

The proprietor or clerk looks at all the cards filed for attention at the beginning of each business day, and checks them against the ledger. If the bill has been paid and is noted in the ledger, he then pulls the card and destroys it or marks it paid and places it in a back file.

If, however, the bill has not been paid, the card activates the collection system, the letter or telephone call is initiated and the card is filed ahead in the next step of the collection process, after being marked with a notation of this action.

The tickler file system leaves nothing to chance. All delinquent accounts turn up automatically at the crucial time for action. The creditor handles each overdue account regularly and methodically. The plan demands little work and saves time and money.

The only disadvantage to the plan is that it duplicates records and becomes an additional clerical job. But this is a small drawback to a method that keeps money coming in and prevents the accidental disregard of a long-delinquent account.

THE DUPLICATE-INVOICE SYSTEM

The duplicate-invoice system resembles the card-tickler system in several aspects, but works in almost exactly the opposite manner. For each bill sent out to the debtor, an extra copy is kept in a duplicate file. When the bill is paid, the extra copy is destroyed. The invoices for bills left unpaid remain in the duplicate file. These become, in effect, the overdue notices in the card-tickler system.

Duplicate copies of bills are filed in a tickler file with thirty-one compartments, so that each duplicate appears on the due date for action. The file can be arranged so that the duplicate invoice of the unpaid bill appears a day or two *before* the due date, if the creditor wishes.

When the invoice appears, the creditor checks it against the ledger. If the bill has been paid, the duplicate is destroyed or filed in a back file. If the bill has not been paid, it then becomes a tickler file card and activates the collection system. It is then returned to the file (as in the card-tickler system) on the date of the next step in the collection campaign.

It is obvious that the card-tickler system is easier to operate than the duplicate-invoice system, and takes up less room. However, the duplicate-invoice system is preferable in a business environment where more accounts fall overdue than are paid up on time. If most of the invoices are quick-pay, the duplicate system becomes ponderous and redundant. Keeping track of the paid bills as well as the unpaid bills is a nuisance.

OTHER FOLLOW-UP SYSTEMS

There are obviously many variations on these three basic systems. Each creditor should look carefully at the possibilities and adapt one for his own special use—one that will work best for the business or service involved.

One way to provide the very best system now in operation is to automate all billings, accounts receivable and collection systems. In other words, to computerize the entire financial process. With computers now available in all sizes, shapes and price ranges, it is the obvious way to go—even for the small businessperson or professional.

It's an entire new way of thinking. Shopping for a computer can be a grand adventure or a spectacular disaster. The ins and outs are complicated. The next chapter is devoted to setting up a computerized billing and collecting system and to a systematized method of shopping around for the proper hardware and software to operate it.

CHAPTER FIVE

Computerizing The Collection System

Bookkeeping—all the way from keeping the records straight to billing and collecting overdue accounts—is fundamentally a matter of filing and retrieving information. The information is amounts of money, along with lists of names of people who owe money and to whom money is owed. A ledger is a simplified filing system that contains these amounts for easy reference.

The collection systems outlined in the previous chapter are all based on this simple method of filing information for retrieval at a certain time and for a certain reason. It is obvious that these mechanical processes almost beg for automation. One of the principal functions of today's computer is filing and retrieving—in other words, the input and output of data in a controlled fashion.

It is no surprise that many business offices have already computerized their billing and collection functions to create good, workable systems.

WHEN THE PRICE IS RIGHT

The good news for the small businessperson, the professional and the individual proprietor is that the cost of computers has rapidly decreased in the past few years, making it possible for a business of almost any size to utilize the resources of computer science to automate all financial systems.

For a large corporation, computerization involves the creation of billing, accounts receivable and collection systems that are individual and that fulfill specific needs for the firm employing them. Such *programming*, as it is called, is expensive and takes time to develop.

For the small company, the computer industry has devised a number of *applications programs*, which are pre-fabricated programs available inexpensively with the functions already written out in special software language. These programs can operate almost all types of personal computers.

By using these applications programs and by preparing a series of collection letters (discussed in Chapters Seven through Thirteen) the small businessperson can automate an office so that the computer keeps the books, types out and sends the bills, spots overdue accounts and types and sends collection letters!

It's not magic. It's just the computer age.

The following material is supplied as a basic guide to understanding and to shopping for a computer to provide financial automation.

THE FUNCTIONS OF THE COMPUTER

The computer's three basic functions in its primary role as an information-processing machine are:

- Storage and retrieval of information
- Performance of arithmetic computations: addition, subtraction, multiplication and division
- Comparison values, numerical or alphabetical, to

see if they are equal, or if one is greater than the other.

By combining these basic functions, the computer can also:

- Classify data
- Sort out names or numbers
- Calculate arithmetic functions
- Summarize numerous transactions in one overall computation
- Store information for future reference.

Data must first of all be organized. A computer's data system is called a *field*. A collection of fields is called a *record*. A grouping of records is called a *file*. Data organized to support the information is called a *data base*.

The computer itself is only a part of the total operation. The machine is called *hardware*, and the program of instructions that runs it, *software*.

COMPUTER HARDWARE

There are several major elements of hardware involved in a computer system:

- Computer, the heart of the hardware
- Disk storage, the memory, where the data is filed
- Terminal, where input and readout occur
- Keyboard, where the operator feeds input
- Cathode-ray tube (CRT), or monitor, where input and output can be read
- Printer, the device that types readout material

HOW THE COMPUTER WORKS

The computer works only with data broken down into what is called *binary* form. A binary system of mathematics uses only two modes: zero and one. Electric current that runs a computer either flows or it doesn't; it is "on" or "off." The presence of electrical current represents 1; the absence, 0. Any number, letter or mark of punctuation is coded into a series of ones and zeros to communicate with the computer. A pattern *10001101* means something to the computer; each zero or one is called a *bit* (binary digit). Each *word* in computerese is a series of eight or sixteen bits; eight or sixteen bits becomes a *byte*. And each byte becomes a specific letter or figure as we recognize it.

The memory of a computer is measured in kilobytes. A kilobyte is roughly 1000 (kilo; K) bytes (actually, a kilobyte equals 1024 bytes). A computer with 64K of memory can store 65,536 bytes; 64K of memory is usually considered 64,000 bytes.

The computer is composed of four main internal components:

- Microprocessor chip, the central processing unit (CPU), which runs the computer
- Electronic clock, which synchronizes operations
- Read-only memory (ROM), the permanent storage of data and programs
- Random-access memory (RAM), used for temporary storage and processing.

The operator communicates with the computer through what is called an input-output (I/O) device, such as the CRT keyboard. This device is called an interface; it is a link between computer components.

INPUT AND OUTPUT OF INFORMATION

The most visible part of any computer is the video terminal, usually a simple television-type screen (cathode-ray tube; CRT). The screen is also called the *monitor* in computer language. The next most visible piece of equipment is the keyboard, usually attached directly to the monitor. Similar to a typewriter keyboard, it is provided with extra keys to perform special functions in operating the computer.

The CRT and keyboard are operated together as the terminal to provide a means of feeding information and instruction into the computer and of calling up information out of the computer on the monitor or on the printer.

The average CRT usually provides a "page" of information twenty-four lines deep, with each line eighty characters long. Most monitor screens are twelve inches wide.

In simple language, the monitor and keyboard provide essentially the same kind of service a typewriter with a sheet of paper rolled into it provides; the operator feeds information into the CRT as the typist feeds information onto the paper.

However, the keyboard performs other duties. The operator can call up information out of the computer memory on the monitor, and can also instruct the computer to perform other functions by punching certain keys.

HOW THE COMPUTER STORES DATA

The most important part of the computer, its memory, is hidden from view. Without the memory, there would be no point in having or in using a computer. A computer memory is divided into two separate parts: the main memory and the auxiliary memory.

The *main memory* is built into the computer. It operates the entire system. It tells the computer what to do by means of instructions communicated by the keyboard. The main memory usually is large enough to handle about 64K bytes. Almost 10K bytes are taken up with operational instructions, leaving the balance for input or processing.

Because the size of a computer's memory is so important, it can be expanded from the 64 bytes into a much larger capacity. This added memory, containing a great deal of storage space, is callecd an *auxiliary memory*. It can be added in at least two different forms.

One type of added memory is the floppy disk or floppy diskette. This disk is thin, flexible and plastic; it can store additional memory from 150,000 up to 340,000 bytes on each side.

Another type of added memory is a disk that is large, hard and rigid. This disk can store up to 275 million bytes, but usually contains about 100 million or so. (**Comparison:** A disk storing 10 million bytes of data can handle roughly 5000 pages of double-spaced typewriting.)

No disk containing added storage space for memory operates by itself. A disk drive is required to link up the memory disk with the computer. Early personal computers used single-drive systems; now most use dual-drives. A dual-drive enables the operator to move data from one storage disk to another at will, increasing the operator's options.

HOW THE PRINTER WORKS

In addition to the monitor, the keyboard, the disk drive and the computer, the typical system uses a printer. It is the function of the printer to receive data in the form of electrical impulses from the computer memory and type out the data on paper.

There are several different kinds of printers. A dot printer, called also a matrix printer, is usually adequate for someone who does not need letter-perfect copy. The letters appear as tiny dots sprayed on the paper.

For letter-perfect copy, which is recommended for office use, the daisy-wheel printer is usually preferred. The daisy-wheel—so called because it is flat and round like a daisy blossom—delivers print that is exactly like typewriter type.

COMPUTER SOFTWARE

Simply put, the software in a computer tells the hardware what to do. In short, the *software* of a computer is the *program* that makes it run. It is usually much less expensive than the hardware. There are now available many hundreds of programs for businesspersons, including software that can handle most bookkeeping processes. (**Important Note:** Although it might seem logical to purchase a computer by studying the monitor

44

and the keyboard first, then looking at the printer, nothing could be less logical. The first and most important consideration is the program! The software always will dictate the kind of hardware you must have. Of the hardware, the most important consideration is the effective storage space for data, in other words, the auxiliary memory, or disk drive. Monitor, keyboard and printer come last, although letter-perfect printing is a must if letters and statements are involved in the computer's work.)

Software usually comes in the form of a magnetic floppy disk, along with a booklet describing the package's features and uses. Usually a preprogrammed package does not fit exactly into the system a buyer wants, but it is close enough for slight modification of the system to fit the applications package.

The typical prepackaged program might handle accounts receivable, general ledger and even general bookkeeping.

For example, the billing program might help process orders more easily and mail invoices faster, stimulating cash flow. Typical billings functions might be:

- Selective printing of invoices
- Calculation of discounts, taxes or special handling
- Pricing of inventory items.

The accounts-receivable program might help provide customers with clear records of payment, maintain up-to-date accounting files and control collections. Typical functions:

- Automatically aged accounts
- Detailed records of charges and payments
- Multiple general-ledger distributions of each invoice
- Application of full or partial payments to selected invoices.

The typical general-ledger program might help reduce time spent on clerical accounting tasks. Functions:

- General-ledger reports showing effect of each account

45

- Trial-balance reports
- Balance sheets
- Income statements.

A SYSTEM OF COLLECTION LETTERS

In addition to performing the functions of keeping the books accurately and spotting overdue accounts, the computer can also help the individual proprietor in expediting one of the most important elements of the typical collection system—the preplanned and carefully orchestrated series of collection letters (see Chapters Nine through Thirteen).

Using the capabilities of the computer in word processing, the creditor can create a series of collection letters which gradually increase in intensity, and file them in his own collection file. Then, when the applications program isolates an overdue account, he simply calls up the proper collection letter, inserts the name of the customer and causes it to be typed and mailed.

To have this capability, the computer must have a printer and sufficient memory to store a series of letters.

SHOPPING FOR THE RIGHT COMPUTER

For a medium-sized firm, it is obvious that too small a computer is not going to work effectively; it is also obvious that for a small firm, too large a computer is a waste of money. The shopping problem is to zero in on the right price.

Basically, computers for business applications fall into three different price ranges:

- *Low-End Computer.* The price of hardware and software to do financial modeling, budgeting and planning can be as low as $3000. The choice of such a model depends on the number of clients or customers involved in the business.

- *Middle-Range Computer.* The price of hardware and software to accomplish the financial applications mentioned above and to do general ledger, accounts receivable, accounts payable, inventory and payroll, runs somewhere around $5000. This is personal computer territory. Again, the choice depends on the amount of inventory, number of customers and so on.

- *Top-Range Computer.* For a relatively large firm, hardware and software usually cost $10,000 and more, with a typical software program running around $3000.

WHAT SIZE COMPUTER TO ORDER?

It is a good idea to calculate in advance the number of letters and figures needed in a typical invoice, billing or collection letter. That is, a typical accounts-receivable record might require 300 characters; that would include 120 characters for the name, address and additional information; another 120 for year-to-date data; and forty for the current balance. With 500 customers, the storage space needed will come to at least 150,000, or 150K bytes. (**Note:** The system that boasts of 64K bytes exhausts about 10K in its main memory; a typical applications package [the program], uses up another 15K; that leaves only 39K for processing. In such a case, it would be advisable to incorporate an auxiliary memory [disk storage] of 120,000 bytes at least. The most formidable cost involves disk storage; without proper room for storage, the system will not work effectively anyway.)

In order to go out shopping for the right computer, the individual proprietor should not only calculate figures like the above, but have in hand the proper numbers relative to the business. There are key questions to ask the computer representative. A typical list might include:

- *How many customers?* This figure will help the salesperson to estimate the size of file necessary.

47

- *How many customers month-by-month?* This figure can show anticipated growth, letting the salesperson suggest hardware and software that can allow for growth.
- *How many statements are written each month?* This question can give the computer representative an idea of the amount of data entry, file size and printing load needed.
- *What is the frequency of aged trial balance?* This can give the salesperson an idea of the amount of printer load.
- *How many invoices each week?*
- *How many lines per invoice?*

Prices vary in the computer business. Several years ago, the cost for one computer was much too high for even a middle-sized firm to handle. Now, even the smallest business can afford some kind of computerized help. The quick growth of the personal computer (PC) in the past several years attests to the fact that almost anyone can be a prospective customer. Such a machine can cost from $3000 to $7000. The high sales of software programs in the financial and business field are proof of the effectiveness of the computer in maintaining proper billing and in stepping up collections.

CHAPTER SIX

Time Schedule for Overdue Accounts

Second in importance to devising a foolproof system for discovering immediately when an account or bill is overdue is the need to establish a fair time schedule to determine the speed with which requests for payment should be made.

Currently, most businesses allow about thirty days for the normal payment of a bill. In some special cases, depending on the business and the situation, only fifteen days are allowed. With the thirty-day account, the money is due on the thirty-first day from delivery; with a fifteen-day account, on the sixteenth day.

However, delays in the postal system mean that many payments may be received not much before thirty-five or forty days from the date of delivery of goods or service.

OVERLAPPING OF WORKING AND BILLING

One problem becomes immediately evident. If the creditor ships his commodities or performs his services on a monthly basis, the bill for January's produce or work usually won't be paid until the middle of March, or later. That is, the money will be coming in probably forty-five days from the date of delivery or performance. While the January bill is waiting to be paid, the February work is on its way or being performed.

A creditor must set up a system that *reminds* the debtor of the bill on the thirty-first day so that payment will be in the mail at least within thirty days of receipt of the bill. If the cross-over causes problems, the creditor should then set back the time period between performance and billing to fifteen days, rather than thirty.

A steady, good-risk customer deserves more understanding and less harsh treatment than the slow-pay customer, even when a delay is unexpected. It is always advisable for the creditor to make certain whether or not the bill has become misplaced or delayed—even lost!—in the mail.

FIRST ACTION TO TAKE ON UNPAID BILLS

When an account remains uncollected for a time, most creditors charge interest on the overdue amount. The time at which such a charge is originally levied varies from one company to the next. Usually no attempt should be made to collect interest on an ordinary open account until it remains uncollected for a substantial period of time.

However, when a bill continues to remain unpaid, the creditor should add an interest charge. In every such case, notice of intent should be made beforehand so that the debtor will not be unhappily shocked when the added charge is announced. Such a notice can be printed on all statements, included in stickers attached to bills or made a part of the original understanding when the account is opened.

GRACE PERIODS

For delinquent accounts that are not settled after many weeks, some firms have a cut-off date after which the creditor cuts off further credit until payment is made. Usually a grace period is given before the creditor suspends all credit.

The period may vary from thirty to ninety days, depending on the size of the bill, on the amount of goods or service involved or on the particular kind of goods or service. The period also varies from individual to individual; some creditors are stricter than others in consideration of arrears. The procedure varies during different financial situations, that is, longer periods during recessions or slow business, and shorter periods during prosperity and good times.

HOW OFTEN TO DUN FOR OVERDUE MONEY

In an article entitled "Effectively Manage Receivables to Cut Costs" in the January-February 1981 edition of the *Harvard Business Review,* Stephen D. Popell advised: "When formulating your collection policies and procedures, remember that firmness and consistency are far more important than fairness. Let your competitors settle for an average age of fifty to seventy-five days. You should strive for thirty days and should settle for no more than forty-five days. All it takes is an early start and dogged determination."

AT THE END OF 30 DAYS

A suggested calendar of procedure drawn up according to this formula of aggression and consistency shows that collection activity should begin at the end of thirty days, without fail. It is suggested that the communication of this reminder be performed by telephone and/or by letter. The import of the message is that the account is overdue, and the debtor is asked to pay. No other action is recommended at this time.

AT THE END OF 45 DAYS

At the end of forty-five days, a *second* letter and/or telephone call is required. The import of this communication is a request that the debtor pay up the invoice or bill within fifteen days; if not, the creditor will stop shipment of goods or the performance of service. Other than this message, no action is recommended.

AT THE END OF 60 DAYS

Fifteen days later, at the end of sixty days, a third telephone call and/or letter is suggested. The import of that communication is to inform the debtor that the creditor has stopped all shipments of goods to the debtor. In more firm tones, the message is made clear: pay *now!* On this sixtieth day, action should be taken. The creditor puts a stop to further shipments of material or performance of service.

AT THE END OF 75 DAYS

After another fifteen-day interval, the fourth letter and/or telephone call is scheduled. This message is even more firm and assertive. The creditor tells the debtor, in no uncertain terms, to pay up . . . or else. If the payment is not received within fifteen days, the creditor will turn over the account for collection. An alternative is to take the unpaid bill to small claims court. The creditor can hire an attorney to take care of collection. No other action is recommended. Note that the *threat* of court, collector or attorney is the extent of the message. A loophole is afforded for payment.

AT THE END OF 90 DAYS

At the end of three months—on the ninetieth day—a fifth letter is sent out; no telephone call is necessary. This letter specifically says that the creditor is taking the action previously cited in the fourth communication—collections agency, small claims court, attorney. And at that time the action specified is definitely taken.

THE KEY ELEMENT IN COLLECTIONS

"The essential element is consistent implementation of your collection policies," Popell points out. "Once a receivable is past due according to your published terms, you have more right to the money than your customer does.

"Get to know the individuals who can influence how quickly you will be paid. Let them know that yours is a small company and that quick turnover of money is critical for your success," suggests Popell.

In a small company, the people responsible for paying the bills are usually the president, the controller or the bookkeeper. In a large company, that is usually the accounts payable department. The creditor should find out who actually processes the bills.

THE IMPORTANCE OF LETTERS AND CALLS

Basic to any collection system is the use of letters, telephone calls and personal visits. The writing of collection letters is tricky, but necessary. It takes a knowledge and understanding of psychology as well as an understanding of legal problems involved in slander and libel. There are also numerous barriers erected against collection procedures by the federal government.

The three-month collection plan discussed above is actually divided into several distinct phases of development: notification of an overdue bill; reminder of an overdue bill; discussion of an overdue bill (how to settle it, for example); urgent action to be taken.

The key points to note are (1) the initial notice of an overdue bill, and (2) the final stage of urgency just before action must be taken. Between these points there are a variety of pleas that can be made, different methods of payment that can be discussed and certain actions that can be taken to persuade the debtor to pay up the overdue account.

DEVELOPING AND RUNNING A SYSTEM

It takes a real understanding of human nature to originate, develop and run a successful collection system. In addition to the proper basic structure, it takes skill and psychological know-how to determine what type of collection appeal to use in each situation. The proper selection of collection elements depends on the ability to "read" a debtor's psychological profile, along with consideration of his past credit record and other factors.

Such a system contains a maze of various time limits on installment payments, procedures regarding consumer credit and collections and so on.

A true and effective collection policy is based on several key points:

- Bringing the debt to the debtor's attention promptly and regularly
- Using increasing firmness as the past-due period lengthens
- Timing reminder messages according to debtor reliability
- Knowing what to say in each message
- Being aware of the differences in each debtor's situation
- Understanding that each type of credit account varies
- Being completely aware of the various legal aspects involved in collection methods
- Working within the parameters of the system and its policies.

Psychological attitude in creating collection messages is extremely important in dealing with debtors. Courtesy, consideration, tact, fairness, a positive point of view and, above all, firmness without rigidity, are needed. The creditor must understand human nature and how to appeal to the debtor's own psychological makeup.

It is rather like a juggling act to balance the severity of a collection appeal with a debtor's past payment record, while keeping within the parameters of the collection system—and within government regulations—yet it must be done.

CHAPTER SEVEN

The Four Stages of The Collection System

Typically the collection system is divided up into four separate stages. Each stage involves several specific efforts, or collection endeavors. Some efforts are interchangeable from one stage to another; others are not. However, the successful system contains a series of efforts in various stages of follow-up which increase in intensity the longer overdue the account or bill becomes.

The choice of each particular effort is governed by the various steps that are taken in each stage, particularly in their suitability to the special collection effort of the client, customer or user.

THE FOUR STAGES OF COLLECTION

Essentially, the four different stages are The Nudge, The Appeal, The Push and The Squeeze.

THE NUDGE

The first stage is actually divided into two separate phases. The first phase is called the *notification phase;* the second is called the *reminder phase.*

Notification phase. This is the point at which the creditor notifies the debtor that the account is overdue. Notification usually takes place at the end of thirty days from the due date of the bill or account.

Reminder phase. This is the point at which the creditor begins to send out reminders to the debtor of the overdue account. The reminder phase usually begins at about forty-five days from the due date of the account.

During the first stage—The Nudge—the creditor assumes that the debtor has made an honest mistake and has simply overlooked the bill in question. The tone of the printed cards, letters or other reminders, including telephone calls, are objective, unemotional and impersonal. (Chapter Twelve discusses The Nudge in detail, with examples of the various collection endeavors and efforts available.)

During The Nudge, the creditor usually relies on printed forms or letters to communicate his notification and reminders to the debtor of his indebtedness.

Because the letter and other forms of written communication are so important, Chapter Eight will discuss what the creditor should include in such a letter, and Chapter Nine is a crash course in letterwriting techniques in general.

THE APPEAL

The second stage is also divided into two separate phases, although the phases are not separated by time so much as by function. The phases, or facets of the stage, are *the appeal* and *the discussion.*

The appeal. One phase of stage two—The Appeal—is the use of various emotional appeals to the debtor to inspire him to pay his overdue debt. These include appeals to sympathy, to pride, to justice, to self-interest and even to fear. The use of several appeals in the composition of collection letters is an important but complex subject, dealt with in detail in Chapters Thirteen and Fourteen.

The discussion. In addition to the use of appeal to the emotions, stage two also involves trying to persuade the debtor to sit down to discuss the nonpayment of debt with the creditor. For that reason, stage two is sometimes called the discussion stage.

Nevertheless, both elements of stage two—appeals and discussions—are motivating factors in the creditor's communications with the debtor.

The Appeal is the most lengthy and complex stage of all four collection stages. It usually involves a longer time span as well. Starting about forty-five days from the due date of the account, it may stretch out another forty-five.

While stage one usually involves only printed or written communications, stage two can also involve individually written letters, personal visits and telephone calls. Confronting the debtor in person is the most effective way to deal with an overdue account, yet it is not always feasible. The telephone call is a suitable substitute. (See Chapter Ten for discussion of telephone calls and personal visits.)

In stage two, collection letters become even more complex and subtle, so that not only does the appeal for discussion change considerably, but the dangers of libel and slander must be considered. (See Chapter Eleven for a discussion of libel and slander.) No second-stage collection letters should be posted without a clear understanding of what constitutes libel.

During stage two, the creditor can resort to action, especially that of cutting off credit to the debtor. (See Chapter Thirteen, which covers the methods of communication and techniques of action in The Appeal.)

During the second stage, the creditor assumes that the debtor recognizes his delinquency, but either will not or cannot pay it. The creditor uses a wide range of methods of communication, emotional appeals and actions to try to bring about a personal discussion of the overdue account or to persuade the debtor to pay up.

THE PUSH

The third stage, The Push, follows the total collapse of all stage-two efforts. By the time all the various avenues of The Appeal have been pursued to no avail, the creditor finally gives up his personal attempts to bring about a discussion and a resolution of his debt and threatens to turn everything over to a professional collector, a lawyer or the small claims court.

This stage—The Push—usually occurs on about the ninetieth day from the due date of the account, although in some instances it can be much later than that. The Push is also called the "urgency" stage, for obvious reasons. (Chapter Fourteen discusses the technical details of The Push. The creditor has the option of various methods to implement this specific "push" action.)

THE SQUEEZE

The fourth stage occurs after The Push has failed to motivate the debtor to pay off his debt. By now the collection system has moved through all of its more elaborate phases. Because gentle reminders, pleas for discussion and even threats have failed to elicit response from the debtor, the creditor now shifts gears, so to speak, and enjoins the legal apparatus for help in getting his money.

The Squeeze is really—and simply—collection by legal effort. In effect, it spells failure for the creditor's collection system, for his nonlegal efforts to extract payment by cajolery, pleas and psychology. It is a sequel to the collection process. Several avenues are open to the creditor: he can go to small claims court himself and sue; he can put his overdue account in the hands of a professional collector; or he can turn the account over to an attorney.

The difference between the first and third options, though seemingly small, is actually significant. When a creditor makes use of the small claims court, he is using the legal system as a layman, usually without the help of a lawyer (although he *can* be represented in small claims court by an attorney if he wishes). If the claim is less than $1000, an attorney's fees are usually too high to warrant his employment. (Three chapters—Fifteen, Sixteen and Seventeen—discuss these three avenues of legal action: first in the small claims court, then through a collection agent and then in the hands of an attorney.)

The Squeeze usually takes place after the account has been overdue ninety days.

SETTLEMENT DURING THE FOUR STAGES

Naturally, the creditor may not need to move to The Appeal at all. His debtor may pay up the overdue bill during the notification or reminder phase of stage one. Or he may pay up during The Push.

Not all debts are paid up in full and in a single move. Many are broken up into two, three or four payments. The settlement may be made by promissory note, which means that the debtor simply pays the bank interest on a loan, with the bank advancing the money to the creditor. There are, in fact, a number of methods by which a creditor and a debtor can work out the settlement of a debt which the debtor finds too onerous or too big to pay off at the time.

These options are discussed in detail at the end of Chapter Thirteen.

Once the settlement is made, the collection process is suspended.

CHAPTER EIGHT

The Collection Letter: Heart of the System

There are three ways to collect overdue money: to make a personal visit and ask for it face to face; to telephone the person who owes the money and ask for it; or to write a letter pointing out that the money is overdue and requesting payment by return mail.

The most effective is the first method. One-on-one confrontation has an impact and a value that cannot be duplicated by telephone or letter. However, for the busy merchant, professional or individual proprietor, this procedure may not be practical. It takes the creditor away from his business. It wastes hours of time—wasted in the sense of taking time away from work. It may not be feasible at all if the debtor lives or works far away.

For those reasons, the most effective method of collecting money has become the least used.

A telephone call has the advantage of taking a relatively short time and of keeping secretarial (letter-writing) fees to a minimum, but it can also be time-consuming. In fact, the debtor may be difficult to locate; he may actually be hiding out. Telephoning is less frequently used in collecting overdue bills than writing letters. However, it is used frequently as a backup to a collection letter.

Although it is only third in effectiveness to the personal visit and the telephone call, the collection letter has become the most common of all three methods. It is simple; it is easy to handle; it can be integrated into a workable collection system or even be computerized.

The purpose and the psychological set of the collection letter will be discussed first, and then a short, crash program in writing the collection letter will follow. After that, the preplanning involved in the personal visit and the telephone call will be discussed in detail.

THE TWO-FOLD PURPOSE OF THE COLLECTION LETTER

Although the average creditor may think the primary purpose of a collection letter is specifically aimed at getting money owed, the *real* purpose is somewhat different. It is to collect the money, but at the same time to keep the customer's good will.

The fact that the purpose is two-fold makes the creation of a collection letter a bit complicated. To write a good letter, the creditor must not only have an understanding attitude about the creditor-debtor relationship, but must also understand exactly how to reflect his concern about the lateness of payment.

Each collection letter in a series must be couched in exactly the right language and tone in order not to anger the debtor with excessive pressure or to make him feel he is off the hook with too little pressure. The key to finding the right "voice" in which to write the letter is the ability to understand the debtor's feelings and to be able to use them to persuade him to *want* to pay.

A debtor may be concerned about his unpaid bill even though he makes no move to pay it or even to admit that it exists. As it becomes more and more overdue, his concern may increase to a point where he becomes despondent and fears he may never be able to get enough money to settle up. In this situation, the debtor is caught in a psychic impasse; he can move neither forward nor backward. He is stuck on dead center.

The creditor must never allow a debtor to feel unable to move; in other words, the creditor must be sure that he does not make the debtor feel backed into a corner. It is the instinct of the cornered individual—man or beast—to fight when trapped. The debtor fights by refusing to pay his debt or by concocting scenarios to prove that he never owed the money in the first place.

To put the debtor in such a spot is the last thing any creditor wants to do. He wants the debtor to feel able to move in any direction; the creditor must make the debtor anxious to pay.

The only *proper* attitude for the creditor to take is to assume that the debtor *will* pay. The only *proper* move for the creditor to make is to have at hand a choice of collection appeals to use, to have at hand a complete record of the debtor's credit history and to be able to strike exactly the right tone in appealing to the debtor's integrity. Essentially, what the creditor must do is understand human nature and be able to play the debtor exactly the way a skilled fisherman plays a fish on a hook. (See Chapter Eleven for a discussion of legal entanglements that can occur during the collection process. The creditor must always work within the legal system in trying to persuade the debtor to pay his account.)

THE PROBLEM OF HUMAN NATURE

It is quite easy for the beleaguered creditor to look on the unpaid bill as an entity in itself, without any human attachment. One of the first rules of writing collection letters is to remember that the recipient of the letter has his own problems, prejudices, perceptions, attitudes and unique outlook. If the debtor is treated with insults, sarcasm or tasteless epithets, he will react with similar expressions of anger. The rule is to avoid as much as possible even the *intimation* that the debtor is deliberately trying to weasel out of his obligations.

In writing a collection letter, the creditor must assume that the debtor wants to pay his bills in a conscientious way. Obviously, something has come up that prevents him from doing so. Therefore, the collection letter should begin with a simple reminder that assumes the debtor has overlooked the bill.

Many honest debtors will immediately write or telephone if they find it impossible to pay a bill on time. Conditions in business and even personal problems may make it impossible to meet the settlement on time. A short-term extension of the debt is usually in order at that time.

EVEN THE DEADBEAT IS HUMAN

On the other hand, some debtors pay no attention to reminders, to pleas or to any kind of exhortations. They are pathological deadbeats. Fortunately, they are in the minority. Yet they cause the most trouble for the honest creditor.

Even so, the creditor should always remember that even a deadbeat is a human being. A courteous, tactful attitude will always collect more money from the fringe debtor than anger or intemperance—so long as the attitude is backed up with firmness and patience.

Another important rule in writing a collection letter is to know how and when to try to find out the reason the debtor hasn't paid his bill. Many debtors are sensitive about lack of cash and will not admit that they are strapped for money. Other debtors are unable to manage their funds and continually find themselves in debt, seeking ways to escape. Many of these people can be shown how to budget their cash flow and arrange terms of payment.

In writing collection letters it is essential to avoid certain phrases that wave a red flag in front of the debtor's eyes. Such expressions as "you are delinquent," or "you are in arrears by two months," or "the delinquency of this account" and so on are offensive to many debtors. The simple phrase, "past due," has a gentler, less strident sound.

SETTING THE PROPER TONE AND ATTITUDE

Even in a letter dunning a debtor for an unpaid bill, the creditor is really writing a *sales* letter. The creditor is trying to sell the debtor on the idea that he must pay up quickly. The creditor should honestly try to see things from the debtor's point of view.

"It will be advantageous to you if you can pay as soon as possible," is a much better way to state the idea than the other way around: "It would be inconvenient for us to allow you to remain delinquent."

One of the key methods in setting the proper tone in any collection letter is to look for the best possible character and personal attributes in the debtor. Expressions like "We are confident that . . . ," "You are probably wondering how you can . . . ," "You will agree, I believe, that . . . ," put the situation on an upbeat note.

A phrase in praise of a debtor should single him out; a phrase of criticism of a debtor should be aimed at a larger body of people.

Praise: "You have always paid your bills to us on time."

Criticism: "Yet, at times, many customers unknowingly allow their bills to lapse."

The creditor must try to shield the debtor's pride.

Not: "If you have read our original contract, you know that each bill must be paid within thirty days, no matter what contingencies develop."

But: "Our commitment for bills is always thirty days. Matters sometimes become complicated so that these payments cannot be met."

The creditor should consider the debtor on the same level; it is inadvisable to talk down to him.

Like this: "Thank you for taking the time to tell us your

problems in cash flow. We always appreciate . . . ."

Not this: "We are willing to consider an extension."

CHOICES FOR COLLECTION APPEALS

Certain collection letters discussed later (Chapters Thirteen and Fourteen) involve efforts to persuade the debtor to cooperate in trying to pay even part of an overdue account. Persuasion involves the use of certain appeals to the debtor. There are ways to use appeals favorably; these should be studied and adapted to the individual creditor's collection plan.

Generally, there are two types of appeal: the positive appeal and the negative appeal. Both have their special uses.

The positive appeal is based on the hope for cooperation and for fair play. It appeals to the sympathy, pride and sense of justice of the debtor. When the positive appeal fails to stir the debtor to action, a negative appeal is used. This is an appeal to the debtor's sense of self-interest and fear for himself and his loved ones.

THE EFFECTIVENESS OF
THE COLLECTION LETTER

The letter is usually the most powerful weapon in the arsenal of the collection system. A letter can be timely, it can be flexible, it is economic and the right kind of letter has a personality all of its own. It can be used as an individual one-time shot at the target, or it can be used in a series of shots. The tone can be serious, it can be humorous, it can be sent out regularly or intermittently. It can be delivered by messenger, or through the usual routes. Collection can, indeed, be made by a single letter—the *right* one.

CHAPTER NINE

Effective Letter-Writing Techniques

In order to compose a good collection letter, it is necessary to know the fundamentals of letter writing. What seems easy—the composition of a persuasive appeal—is a complex and sometimes difficult undertaking.

Most unsuccessful letter writers have neither studied the craft carefully nor thought about what happens to their letter once it is mailed. The most important moment in the life of a letter is not the moment it is written, but *the moment it is read.*

One question the successful letter writer always tries to answer before beginning a letter is: how will the person to whom the letter is addressed react when he or she opens it and glances at it briefly?

The average businessperson usually goes through the mail in the morning. He or she sorts out the important mail from the unimportant mail, but does it in a fashion that sometimes has nothing to do with the actual *content* of the letters. There is a glance down at the letter, then the recipient automatically puts the letters that look easy to read into the top-priority pile; those that look hard to read are thrust aside for later study—if there ever is a later.

Except for the content of any letter, the most important point in its creation is to make it have good eye appeal, to make it something the recipient *wants* to read.

To go at the problem backwards, there are a number of definite don'ts in the mechanics of letter-writing. Things to avoid in creating an effective letter are often more important than the things one actually does.

SOME IMPORTANT DON'TS

There are a number of warnings any letter-writer should be aware of. The most important of these are:

- Don't crowd any letter too high at the top of the page, too low at the bottom or too close to the margins. Leave at least an inch on all sides. Crowding automatically turns off the reader. A reader always follows the line of least resistance and reads only what looks easy.

- Don't use enormously long and complicated looking paragraphs. Long paragraphs went out with the nineteenth century. Single-spaced paragraphs of over ten lines actually create resistance in even the most astute and intelligent reader.

- Don't use short, choppy paragraphs; they look ridiculous. Each paragraph should state and develop an idea. By stringing out one idea into three or four tiny paragraphs, the thrust of the argument is lost.

- Don't write one-paragraph letters if possible. Even though a good letter is short and easy to read, a blob of type in the middle of the page is a definite handicap to reading. By thrusting a number of different ideas at the reader in one paragraph the writer has created a sure-fire way to lose the reader's attention.

- Don't clutter up a letter with long and convoluted salutations. The name of the recipient, title and address is enough.

SOME IMPORTANT DO'S

After a study of the points above, it is obvious that the importance of any business letter is to look good and to invite reading. Pay attention to these rules:

- Be sure to place the content of the letter in graceful balance in the middle of the page. Confine the letter to one page; it is an unusual subject that needs more paper than that. Avoid being verbose and repetitive. Learn to edit your own letters until they move quickly and finish brightly.

- Confine each paragraph to six lines or less. By the time a paragraph gets to be ten or fifteen lines long, it is virtually unreadable at first glance. A great deal of material in an extra-long paragraph can be condensed or dropped.

- A paragraph is a block of material which develops one specific idea, or several closely related ideas, and confines itself to one overall subject. Sometimes combining two choppy paragraphs gets the idea across much better.

- Consider every letter as having three basic parts: opening, body and closing. Each can take up a separate paragraph. It is the body that sometimes needs more than one paragraph for adequate expression or argumentation.

- Keep both salutation and closing of a letter relatively clean, without adding unnecessary details. The opening and the closing should be crisp, clean and direct.

CONTENT OF THE LETTER

Although mechanics are essential in the production of a successful letter, it is the *content*—particularly in a collection letter—that is the most crucial part of it.

There are at least five main points to the composition of the perfect collection letter, involving the

- Opening
- Style
- Diction
- Tone
- Closing.

THE OPENING

The first paragraph of the collection letter is absolutely crucial. The proper tone must be set in the opening words, the proper attitude must be demonstrated, the proper "set" of mind for the entire letter. If the opening is in any way undiplomatic, the reader is lost. If the opening is tired and stereotyped, the reader is lost.

The creditor must keep five things always in mind when composing those first few words of the collection letter:

- He must arouse the interest of the debtor.
- He must immediately persuade him as to the seriousness of the situation.
- He must pique his interest without putting his back up.
- He must tease him enough to make him want to read the rest of the letter.

- Essentially, he must retain the understanding and friendship of the debtor.

One of the best ways to lose the interest of the debtor is to use hackneyed phrases or clichéd opening statements. For example, these are hackneyed:

- "It has come to my attention. . . ."
- "In checking our records, we find. . . ."
- "We note that you have not. . . ."
- "In reviewing your account at this time. . . ."
- "Thank you for your letter of September 4. . . ."

What's wrong with starting out a letter with a question? One of the reasons a question usually works as an opener is that it automatically arouses the curiosity of the reader and acts as a hook to pull him along into the message. Examples:

- "Could we ask a favor of you?"
- "Is there any way that we can help you?"
- "Will you kindly inform us . . . ?"
- "Can we have your help?"
- "Did our invoice of March 15 go astray?"
- "Have you been away during March and April?"

One of the most important things to remember in writing a collection letter is to use the personal approach at all times. The trick of not being offensive but being firm nevertheless is no easy accomplishment. Note the manner in which the writer of the following opening tempers firmness with tact: "We had sincerely hoped that it would be possible for you to pay your April bill on time. Now that we know of your problem, we can extend the due date fifteen days."

Generally, in an opening:

- Don't use a stereotype
- Don't be long-winded
- Don't be tactless or blunt

- Don't be insulting or libelous
- Try to show appreciation
- Try to be sympathetic
- Try to be reassuring
- Be personal without being overbearing.

THE STYLE

Business letters tend to fall into commercial jargon. Such words are horrendous offenders, turning a basically well-thought-out letter into an unreadable clot of ponderous drivel. Avoid these words:

advise	herewith
attention	indebtedness
above, below, following	investigate
acknowledge	matter
communicate, communication	memorandum
dated	reflects
expedite	respectfully
favor	the undersigned
forward	

Translate these phrases into the *real* meaning:

according to our records	=	our records show
at the present time	=	now
be in a position to	=	can, are able to
business reply envelope	=	envelope
communicate with me	=	write me
complying with your request	=	as you asked
continues to be open against your account	=	remains unpaid
due to the fact	=	as, since
enclosed you will find	=	enclosed is
for this reason	=	thus, so
for your information	=	(leave out)

in the event that	=	if
in the amount of	=	for
in view of the fact	=	since
in reviewing our files we find that	=	we found
in connection with	=	about
in reference to	=	about
information in hand	=	information received
it is our opinion	=	we feel
is due and payable	=	(use either "due" *or* "payable")
in checking your account	=	your account shows
noted in our records	=	recorded
open on our books	=	unpaid
pending receipt of	=	awaiting
to the attention of the writer	=	to me
the above numbered invoices	=	this, these invoices
under date of	=	on (date)
under the circumstances	=	therefore, so
we direct your attention to	=	please notice
we are in receipt of	=	we've received
we do not appear to have received	=	we did not receive

A letter should have a personality of its own, and clichés and jargon blur personality. Note the following letter, with the jargon italicized. Its use obscures the fact that the creditor exists as a person:

> *We direct your attention* to our *previous correspondence, the last being* a letter of September 15, in which *we requested your cooperation* in *forwarding additional remittance* to cover *the above noted balance,* which remains *open on our books.*
> Since the last remittance *the writer* received was

on July 15, in the amount of $75, *it would be appre-ciated* if you would send additional checks *by return mail. Thank you for your cooperation in this matter.*

By using these clichés, the writer obscures his identity, hiding behind a façade of bromides. In fact, he does not appear in the letter; his nonappearance perhaps leading the reader to believe that he does not really mean what he *says* he means. Contrast this request:

> Your time is up . . . and I mean it.
> Since my efforts to help you to pay off your long overdue balance have proved to be unsuccessful, I now have no other choice but to turn your account over to our legal department.

THE DICTION

Diction refers to the ability of a writer to phrase ideas in words that avoid ambiguity, misunderstanding or confusion. By clearing away excess verbiage, bromides and clichés, a writer achieves good diction. In other words, he can state his intentions clearly and avoid being undermined by a ponderous "official" business-letter style.

The essence of letter-writing is to communicate ideas. The human mind works best when it ponders one idea at a time. Cluttered verbiage turns off the mind.

> Not having received then the courtesy of a reply in recent days, or remittance of the account in question, we find it now necessary that we communicate to you the necessity of not allowing the matter of delinquence to go along to an indefinite future date, and unless payment is received promptly and forthwith we shall be unable to adopt any other expedient than to take more drastic steps to protect our interests, which we certainly prefer not to do unless it becomes absolutely necessary.

The letter drafted above has actually four basic ideas:

- The debtor has been written to several times about his overdue invoice, but has failed to answer.
- Unless a check is received immediately, drastic action will be taken.
- The creditor does not want to take such steps.
- A reply should be made without delay.

The main problem in trying to create clear, brief statements on paper is that the unskilled writer immediately uses a cliché or bromide as his anchor. The resulting letter becomes an unfocused string of clichés.

A secondary problem is the skipping back and forth from one idea to another without logical progression. To avoid these letter-writing traps, the writer must first of all determine exactly what he wants to say *before* committing the thought to paper.

Second, the writer must calculate the most effective organization of his thoughts. Once he has made these decisions mentally—of what to say and how to organize it—the actual writing should be relatively easy.

Once the ideas are on paper, he can then go over the sentences, polishing them until they say exactly what he wants, eliminating unnecessary words, adding only those which clarify and eliminate extraneous matters. Ruthlessly delete any long-windedness. Since many letter-writers tend to add unnecessary details, be sure that if details are included, they are used to make important points.

THE TONE

In writing a collection letter, the writer must be constantly on the alert to create the proper "tone." Tone refers to many facets of style—the ability to point out delinquency without alienating the debtor, the ability to initiate action without reprisals, the ability to communicate what you mean without rupturing the relationship.

One of the key elements in creating the proper tone is for the letter writer to think not of his own feelings and emotions—and complaints—but of the recipient's feelings, emotions and possible reactions. In other words, the trick of creating the proper tone in a collection letter is for the creditor always to think of the debtor first and himself second. To establish such a habit will in turn help the creditor to achieve the proper tone in any letter he writes.

An aid in establishing the correct tone is to adopt a "you" attitude, rather than an "I" attitude. A reader loses interest when he feels his problems are being slighted. There is a very simple way to create such a tone in a collections letter: make sure that there are a minimum of "I" and "we" words.

Not this: "We wish to advise you that we are looking into the matter. We will write as soon as we have all the necessary facts."

But this: "It will be a pleasure to send you the information you request in your letter. It should not take more than a few days to assemble this information for you. Meanwhile, thank you for your patience during this delay, and for giving us the opportunity to be of service to you."

By thinking of the recipient of the letter, the creditor can avoid backing the debtor into a corner. A deft collection letter writer always allows the recipient to save face in the matter of being delinquent. (See Chapter Eighteen.) Here are some rules to follow in order not to back the debtor into a corner and make him a permanent enemy:

- Avoid openly contradicting the debtor
- Avoid badmouthing others to build up your case
- Avoid unnecessary arguments of any kind
- Admit any mistakes willingly and immediately
- Avoid cookie-cutting, nit-picking and supercritical remarks
- Avoid sarcasm, bitterness and snide comments
- Avoid presenting yourself as infallible
- Even in a letter demanding payment, try to build good will.

THE CLOSING

The most important moment in the writing of a letter—as in a romantic affair—is the moment of closing it out. The person who successfully breaks off an affair that is lagging is always remembered affectionately; so is the creditor who can wind up a letter adroitly by asking for action without arousing animosity.

The close of a collection letter involves the crux of the problem: it is the paragraph in which the creditor asks for action on the part of the debtor. By the time the problem has been stated and discussed, the debtor knows the details. What he wants to know is what is expected of him.

Such a closing should lay out exactly what the creditor wants the debtor to do, usually within the confines of these three facts: what to do; when to do it; how to do it.

The trick is to do this without offending the debtor.

Thus: "As we are anxious to be of utmost service to you, do let us hear from you promptly about the payment of the $450."

And: "As we don't want to put you to this needless expense and unpleasantness, we shall expect to hear from you within ten days."

A closing can sometimes accomplish much more than simply underlining the action that the creditor wants taken. There are all manner of endings that can be used to create good will, pacify upset debtors, apologize for inconveniences, reassure debtors, reemphasize actions to be taken, summarize the situation, to promote future business and so on.

One key point to remember in phrasing any closing is to leave an opening for the debtor to respond. If the letter does not make it possible for the debtor to answer, by way of explanation, by way of request, by way of pleading, the letter is not a successful piece of writing.

One way to encourage a reply is to include a few simple questions at the bottom of the letter—questions about when payment might be expected, if it would help to have the payment halved, if the recipient wants an extension of the entire account.

Then the final words:

You don't need to write us at all. Just let us know on the questions below when we can expect to receive your payment, and for how much. Return this letter in the envelope attached for your convenience.

For the honest debtor, this type of bait will help bring in at least part of the unpaid amount.

CHAPTER TEN

To Visit or to Call?

If it is at all possible, a creditor should always use the personal visit or the telephone call to work out a solution to an overdue account. However, as has been explained, the collection letter is easily the most common method of handling such difficulties, in spite of its somewhat diminished effectiveness.

The success of a personal visit depends on several factors. Most important is the closeness of the relationship between creditor and debtor. If the two know each other, the visit should be considered definitely friendly and similar to any visit between friends. If the two do not know each other, it must be handled the way an ice-breaking visit between strangers is handled.

A one-on-one dialogue is the best possible way to dispel differences of opinion and to retain the good will of the debtor. Personal communication helps the creditor to "read" the debtor and to shape the collection pitch from moment to moment. If there are difficulties, they usually emerge during the confrontation.

Nevertheless, the creditor should prepare what he is going to say and the way he is going to say it beforehand, more or less outlining his procedure in his own mind before he makes the appointment.

THE DIFFERENT METHODS OF COMMUNICATION

Exactly the same method of preplanning should be incorporated if the creditor intends to make a telephone call to the debtor. Both one-on-one dialogue and conversation by telephone are similar in intent and in execution. The major difference is the lack of eye contact in telephone communication.

Note that while these two methods of communication are different from the written message, there are similarities as well. A written message after all is simply an oral message put down on paper for transportation over a distance. One-on-one dialogue and telephone conversation are more personable and emotionally intense than writing, of course, but the goals, attitudes and procedure are similar.

Currently, increasing use is being made of the telephone in collection systems, particularly in the early and late stages of the process. Telephoning has an advantage over personal visiting; it is easier and takes less time.

By the very nature of communication, in the telephone call and in the personal visit, the creditor can see and hear the directness of the appeal and instantly determine its effectiveness. With written communication, the sender does not know whether or not the message has reached its destination until some time later—if ever.

However, in most cases, it is not wrong for the creditor to use a collection letter first, and then follow that up with either personal visit or telephone call. Both personal visit and telephone call can be used effectively in all stages of the collection process.

PRE-PLANNING THE CALL OR VISIT

A personal visit or telephone call must be well planned in advance in order to be one hundred percent successful.

Four special points must be considered in planning a visit or call ahead of time:

- Determination of purpose
- Understanding of debtor
- Collection of facts
- Note of points to cover.

DETERMINATION OF PURPOSE

Obviously the primary purpose of the collection call is to get overdue money. The secondary purpose is to retain the good will of the debtor. The creditor must go through all correspondence, calls and other notes about the debtor and his account. A study of the debtor's situation may tip off the creditor as to how to handle the dialogue.

In other words, is it the creditor's purpose to work out a special payment arrangement? Is it to remind the debtor of a promise made recently and not kept? Is it to urge the debtor to pay up by a certain date? Is it to present an important decision?

The creditor must have the initial purpose of the call well in mind beforehand.

UNDERSTANDING OF DEBTOR

The creditor must also have a profile of the debtor's character and financial picture in his mind before he sits down to talk to him. The debtor must be the actual person in charge of paying the bills, not an underling, or a ringer from another department. The creditor must understand the debtor's character: is a hard line or a soft line preferable?

The creditor can get a great deal of information about

personality and character from the informational file already on hand. Naturally, the creditor will vary his approach from time to time as the dialogue continues. As the two get to understand one another better, the creditor can increase the pressure on the debtor. Understanding the personality of the debtor is important in trying to figure out how to deal with him or her. Is the debtor short-tempered? easy-going? hostile?

COLLECTION OF FACTS

The creditor must first of all go back through the files to check the facts about the debtor and his situation before planning a strategy. The creditor must also have a good idea of the debtor's past payment record. Is the debtor a deadbeat? Is this his first delinquency? Does it look as if it might simply be a slow season?

Knowing these facts will determine for the creditor whether or not he can suggest a postponement of payment, a partial payment, or even a loan.

NOTE OF POINTS TO COVER

The creditor should write down a list of questions to ask the debtor during the discussion in order to determine the debtor's reasons for not paying his account—if there are any. The questions should be composed in such a fashion that the creditor lets the debtor know that the two of them are on the same side in the matter, and are not adversaries.

However, there is a science to asking verbal questions. The creditor must not allow them to become long and rambling; otherwise, the creditor may end up doing all the talking and the debtor is reduced to saying a simple yes or no. By allowing and inducing the debtor to speak at length, the creditor can then lead him into a suggestion for a settlement.

Good questions—because the very nature of verbal communication is personal rather than impersonal—are the Five Ws: who, what, when, where and why . . . plus how.

It's an old legal axiom never to ask a witness a question

unless the lawyer knows the answer. The same is true of the creditor's questions: he should never ask the debtor how he intends to pay unless he has a payment plan of his own ready to present. That is the key element in the personal or telephone call.

Not only must the payment plan include all overdue bills, but it must feature a specific schedule for payment that will bring the overdue account up to the present. The plan must be simple and understandable. After the call, the plan should be sent to the debtor so it can be studied in print.

THE COLLECTION CALL

Having completed the precall research, the creditor may now consider the elements of the call itself. The successful collection call—personal or by telephone—must be considered as carefully as the well-written collection letter. Tactfully persuasive, it should consist of five primary points:

- Opening statement
- Fact-finding questions
- Presentation of payment plan
- Overcoming of objections
- Closing statement.

THE OPENING STATEMENT

The first thrust of the dialogue belongs to the creditor. It is up to him to come up with a simple, clear, concise statement of the problem. Such a statement usually contains specific information on how much money is due and how long it has been in arrears.

But once that information is conveyed by the creditor, *the creditor must give the debtor time to digest this information.* For this reason, the opening statement is a preliminary discussion only.

At the end of the initial statement, the creditor must pause at least to the count of five before continuing. Usually, that pause will encourage the debtor to make some kind of response. If the debtor is an honest person and wants to pay the debt, he or she will either offer to pay part of it, or all of it, or at least give a reason for *not* paying it.

From this point on, the discussion can be kept on the track until some kind of settlement is offered. That is, the conversation *usually* proceeds in this manner.

FACT-FINDING QUESTIONS

Once the creditor has given his opening statement, and the debtor has responded, the creditor then zeros in on the payment plan envisioned. The discussion can proceed as follows:

The purpose of the preconceived payment plan is to enable the creditor to discuss the pertinent details of the debtor's situation. It may be unrealistic in relation to the debtor's current status. The creditor must be ready to adapt the plan at any point when the debtor either refuses to accept the proposal or points out that such a schedule is impossible to meet.

THE PAYMENT PLAN

The discussion can proceed as follows:

"I've been thinking about your account, and have come up with a plan of action that will get it back on a steady course."

Or, "I'm glad you mentioned that you wish there were a way to get the account back up there without having to do it today. I believe there is. How does this plan sound to you?"

Thus the creditor directs the debtor's attention to the preconceived plan.

If the debtor agrees to discuss a plan, the creditor has been successful in his original aim. Now the creditor continues with the discussion of the details.

OVERCOMING OBJECTIONS

The typical objection to a payment plan is usually the timing of the payments. However, there may be other objections.

There are four basic steps in trying to overcome objections:

- The creditor must find out to what specifically the debtor objects. The objections must be clear in the mind of each before going on.

- The creditor first avoids the points of objection, and gets agreement on the points that are not arguable. The actual objection may be only the date of the payment, for example.

- Once the creditor and debtor agree on a group of points, then the creditor proceeds to the debtor's objections. If they are minor, the creditor can usually compromise on a number of them. However, if the objections are serious, the creditor should look into them more closely to make sure the facts are correct.

- The creditor should remind the customer that paying debts and keeping the account current is a benefit to both parties.

CLOSING STATEMENT

If a plan has been worked out, even only in broad outline, the creditor summarizes the payment plan and thanks the debtor. This leaves the facts clear in the mind of the debtor as well.

> "Let me summarize to make sure I have everything straight. You are going to send me $500 on Friday, August 4. I should have that on the following Monday. You will send another payment of $400 on Friday, August 11. I'll get that on the 14th. And that will bring the account up to date."

DON'TS FOR COLLECTION BY CALL

The creditor should confine his personal or telephone call to working hours. The Federal Communications Commission has laws that cover the use of the telephone, for example, to make tape recording of conversations. In some instances it is illegal to frighten, torment or harass any person by telephone. (Chapter Eleven discusses possible illegalities involved in collection letters and in personal and telephone calls.)

CHAPTER ELEVEN

Caution:
Libel and Slander!

At one time the creditor could go to any extent to collect money from his debtor. It was not so long ago that a debtor might have to serve a term in debtor's prison if he could not pay his bills. Charles Dickens's father was in jail during some years of the boy's life; the future writer had to work to support the family.

The debtor has many more rights today, and certain actions a creditor might be tempted to take are proscribed. He cannot, for example, overstep the laws of defamation, invasion of privacy, fraud, false representation, slander and libel. In effect, the creditor is not allowed to do anything *illegal* to collect his money. Other than that, he is free to act in any way he feels necessary to get his money.

The same latitude does *not* extend to the professional collection agency. Because during the years of extensive credit in the United States, more and more creditors were going to collection agencies to collect unpaid bills, collection agencies became less and less restrained in their attempts to force creditors to pay up bills.

On March 20, 1978, the United States Congress enacted legislation, Fair Debt Collection Practices Act, to protect debtors from the excessive activities of collection agencies. It covers debts incurred for the purchase of cars, medical care and charge-account transactions of all kinds. The law applies *only* to debt collectors—*not* creditors. It does not in any way erase any legitimate debt that a debtor has contracted; it does protect debtors from several types of offensive practices. Among them are these:

- Falsehoods and misrepresentation
- Harassment and abuse
- Unfairness
- Profane, obscene or abusive language
- Character assassination.

ILLEGAL COLLECTION PRACTICES

FALSEHOODS AND MISREPRESENTATION

One favorite trick dreamed up by aggressive collection agents in the past was to imply to the debtor that the agent was an attorney or an agent of the federal or state government working for a credit bureau.

It is no longer legal for a collector to *pretend* or imply that such a fact is true when it is not.

Another favorite ploy was to inflate the amount of the debt owed so that the debtor would think he owed more than he actually did. In some instances the debtor inferred that the debt would continue growing the longer it was not paid off—a situation familiar to a debtor in the grips of a loanshark. Such tactics are no longer permitted.

An agent might twist facts so much that the debtor would infer that he actually had committed a crime by not paying up his debt. Technically, his contract with his creditor was simply an agreement between them; no criminal charges could be brought against him for simple nonpayment of debt. Although a creditor can go to court to *prove* a debt and then instigate legal action to get the money, up to the point of court action the debtor has not committed a crime. Such misrepresentation cannot now be used any longer.

HARASSMENT AND ABUSE

At one time a collection agent might use any number of different threats of violence or harm to the debtor's property, person or reputation. The debtor, accustomed to threats of violence and injury by loan sharks, might seriously fear the same kind of violence. These threats are illegal.

Another effective tactic was for the collection agent to make repeated telephone calls simply for the purpose of annoyance—telephoning without giving full identification, pretending to be an obscene phone caller, telephoning in the early hours of the morning, making abusive threats on the telephone to members of the debtor's family. This, too, is illegal.

The use of obscene language, profane remarks, insults couched in four-letter words—at one time a staple of the collection agent's arsenal of abuse—are no longer allowed.

CHARACTER ASSASSINATION

At one time collection agencies were allowed to publish the names of debtors in order to publicize their delinquency. This particular tactic is no longer allowed agents of collection firms.

In fact, the law protecting debtors against aggressive collection agencies assumes that a debt is a private matter rather than a public matter. The collector cannot in any way broadcast to the public the fact that a debtor owes money. Notices of indebtedness by postcard are no longer allowed. Nor can the agent call the debtor's place of work to discuss his delinquency with his immediate superior or any of his colleagues.

UNFAIRNESS OF VARIOUS KINDS

One of the tactics forbidden by the law is the practice, quite common at one time, of telephoning *collect* to the debtor as a kind of harassment and added nuisance. Nor can the collection agent telephone the debtor at his home between the hours of 9:00 P.M. and 8:00 A.M.

The collection agent cannot discuss the debtor's situation with the debtor's neighbors, his colleagues at work or with his family.

WHAT THE DEBTOR CAN DO

In the event that any debtor believes he has been unfairly treated by a collection agent, he can file a lawsuit and win up to $1000 in penalties, providing the court upholds his claim. In addition to that, the Federal Trade Commission can impose fines of up to $10,000 a day per violation against any overly aggressive bill collector.

WHAT THE COLLECTOR CAN DO

There are many things which the collection agent *can* do. He can still telephone the debtor at his office or home every day and ask for the money that is owed. The agent can even call a neighbor or a friend of the debtor once to ask for the debtor's address or phone number—without mentioning the debt or its amount.

OPTIONS OF ACTION CLOSED TO THE CREDITOR

In general, the creditor himself has many more options open to him in dealing with a debtor than a collection agent. The creditor is not covered by the 1978 statutes protecting the debtor from collection agents. However, the creditor *is* covered by a number of other important legalities. He should know what they are and he should be prepared to abide by them, particularly those pertaining to writing letters, making telephone calls, and dealing with the debtor one-on-one.

Essentially, the particular laws he should be clearly aware of are those in the areas of defamation of character; libel; slander; publication; invasion of privacy; surveillance of records, reports, and letters; fraud and misrepresentation.

DEFAMATION OF CHARACTER

Defamation of character, fame or reputation involves two different kinds of vilification. Defamation by oral communication is *slander*. Defamation by written communication is *libel*. The intentional or negligent communication of defamatory material to a third party is *publication*, and as such is actionable.

The creditor may tell the debtor to his face that he is incompetent, a deadbeat or a swindler; he is within his legal rights. However, if there is a third person in the room, or if the defamatory statement is communicated to one other person (someone who is not a secretary or who is otherwise privileged) the creditor can be in serious trouble. In short, the creditor can be sued by the debtor. Nevertheless truth is the creditor's absolute defense, and proof of his statement can win the case.

The derogatory qualities causing a statement to be defamatory are the same for libel and for slander. Libelous statements are more permanent, and the libel laws are consequently more severe. Libel may involve any permanent communication: letter, postcard, telegram, circular, picture, photograph, cartoon, newspaper, phonograph record or tape. (*Note:* A sealed letter, addressed by a creditor to a debtor, can result in actionable "publication" if the creditor can be shown to have *suspected* that the communication would be

91

intercepted or shown to a third person. For this reason, when a creditor sends a letter to a debtor containing unfavorable information or any message about past-due payments, the communication must be mailed in a sealed envelope and addressed so that it will be read *only* by the person to whom it is addressed. The creditor can help protect himself by adding the words PERSONAL or PERSONAL AND CONFIDENTIAL on the outside in clear bold markings. *Accidental* communication to a third person—by wiretap, eavesdrop or unauthorized reading of a letter—is not actionable. A stenographer or secretary involved in performing the work of producing the letter is considered conditionally privileged and thus cannot be assumed to be a "third person."

A GLOSSARY OF DEFAMATORY TERMS

Some words are libelous and others are not. The line that separates libelous from harmless is often a confusing one. For that reason, the courts continue to be overworked, and lawyers continue to collect large fees.

The sampling below of the most explosive and dangerous words of a defamatory nature should help the creditor to put a padlock on his tongue. These words, unless *true* (truth being an absolute defense in cases of alleged libel), are defamatory on their face. He is warned to avoid them when referring to a person or organization:

bankrupt	incompetent
blackmailer	inferior
Communist	insolvent
corrupt	kickbacks
crook	misappropriation
deadbeat	misconduct
dishonest	misrepresentation
disreputable	profiteer
drug addict	quack
faker	racketeer
falsified	shyster

forger	swindler
fraud (fraudulent)	thief
gouged money	unchaste
grafter	unworthy of credit
hypocrite	worthless

Certain statements become defamatory because they impugn a characteristic necessary in a person's work, that is, because the words attack a person's *professionalism*. For example, it is defamatory to criticize the financial responsibility of a merchant; it is not defamatory to criticize the financial responsibility of a teacher or an opera singer. Reason: the ability to obtain credit is essential only to the merchant. By the same token, it is defamatory to call a public official a Communist, but generally not an engineer or a computer programmer.

In a libel suit, an absolute defense for the accused is proof of the truth of the statement. If the allegedly libeled party is a public figure, the publisher need not even prove the truth of the statement. Absence of malice is then sufficient (*Times* v. Sullivan, 1963). Malice, for the purposes of a libel suite, means publication of an allegation that is knowingly false or careless disregard of its truth or falsity.

INVASION OF PRIVACY

An unreasonable intrusion into the private life of an individual is called *invasion of privacy*. Privacy can be violated even though no publication to a third person takes place, and even though the matters involved are true and not particularly harmful to the reputation. Invasion of privacy is actionable.

It is similar to trespass, which gives a person the legal right to keep intruders off his or her land. Invasion of privacy involves the protection of a mental interest—freedom from mental anguish resulting from an unreasonable intrusion into the person's private affairs.

There are two concepts of invasion of privacy:

- The use of a person's name, picture or other identity without permission
- Physical surveillance of records, reports and letters by persons not entitled to examine them.

In a collection situation, very little use is made of invasion of privacy. Nevertheless, the creditor must be aware of the illegality of searching out records or reports that might belong to the debtor in order to ascertain his financial situation.

FRAUD AND MISREPRESENTATION

The creditor must never lie in his letters to the debtor in any details whatsoever. Nor can any falsehood be *suggested.* Otherwise, the letter may be actionable.

The favorite ploy of the creditor—"I shall be turning your account over to our legal department for collection"—is illegal, *if* the creditor's firm does not actually have a legal department that can handle such collections. If the creditor's firm *does* have a legal department with a proper collection agent, then the statement is not a falsehood.

Even the usual threat of turning the debtor's account over to a collection agency within ten days can be an illegality, particularly if the creditor has no intention of doing so. However, it is difficult for the debtor to *prove* that fact, since the situation can change from day to day, even as the debt continues unpaid.

SUMMATION OF LIBEL AND SLANDER LAWS

The main point of this chapter is to differentiate between the legal right of the *creditor* and the *collection agency.* The creditor obviously has more rights to collect his money from the debtor than the collector does. The obligation is a contract—written or unwritten—between the creditor and debtor. The problem of collection is the creditor's. He has many more recourses open to him than the hired collector acting as his agent.

Nevertheless, there are certain areas where even the creditor can go astray. The main and crucial areas are those of libel, slander and invasion of privacy. A clear concept of what constitutes defamation of character is a must for a creditor who plans to write one or more collection letters for a follow-up system.

CHAPTER TWELVE

The Nudge: Notification and Reminder

The first stage of the collection system, The Nudge, is actually broken up into two distinct and separate phases. One of these phases is that of notification of the overdue debt; the other phase is a series of reminder letters to that effect.

For the sake of discussion, the first stage in the collection system involves all the actions the creditor takes to inform the debtor of the tardiness of an account or bill without taking any other action. The notification and reminders are usually made in the form of written communications or, sometimes, by telephone.

THE ACT OF NOTIFICATION

Many firms send out monthly statements to their customers, but some smaller businesses and individual proprietors do not. For those who have only a few accounts and do not find it necessary to produce a regular monthly statement, the best procedure to follow at the moment a bill or account becomes overdue is to send a duplicate copy of the statement with a stamped notification on it indicating that the account is overdue.

One way to stamp such a bill is with a regular rubber stamp like this:

PAST DUE!
PLEASE SEND CHECK
BY RETURN MAIL

The rubber stamp can take any form, but it should be brief and to the point. Since the action of stamping a bill is in no way a personal act, the use of the stamp does not arouse personal antagonism.

There is an alternative method for the creditor available at this point in the collection process. He can send an individual letter to the effect that the account is overdue. The letter should be completely impersonal and objective. It might read:

> Dear Sir:
> Your bill for $75 was due on January 31. It is now one week overdue. We would appreciate receiving your check by return mail.
> Thank you.

Each letter in a collection series should include the amount due and the account number, if applicable.

Notification is a one-time act. If the bill is not paid after notification, the collection process moves into the second phase of the first stage.

The period of time separating the act of notification and the act of reminders should not exceed fifteen days. By the fifteenth of the month past the thirty days allowed for payment, the bill is definitely overdue, either having been overlooked twice or ignored by the debtor who does not intend to pay.

Once the period of fifteen days is past, the collection system moves into its second step, the reminder phase.

THE REMINDER PHASE

The reminder phase begins at a time the account is definitely overdue and notification of that fact has been sent to the debtor. Measures must be taken now to *remind* the debtor of his unpaid bill. This phase usually involves a series of letters—probably between one and seven—which are simply routine requests for money.

During this phase, the basic assumption of the reminder letter is that the debtor has overlooked the bill and will pay it immediately upon being reminded of the fact.

There are several different types of reminders. They include the following:

- Personal letter
- Impersonal form letter
- Stamped reminder
- Printed form

Of these four types, the most productive is the personal letter, although the creditor may hold it in abeyance until a stamped reminder or a printed form letter has been sent.

THE PERSONAL LETTER

The personal letter might take the form of a relaxed and informal statement of the problem. For example:

Dear Mr. Smith:
In looking through our accounts we note an amount of $348 against your account for the shipment of materials we sent you in January.
Apparently you have overlooked the bill. It would

be a great convenience to us to have your check as soon as possible. We try to keep our records in order.

Would you please send us your remittance? If you have already done so, please excuse our asking.

Very truly yours

THE IMPERSONAL FORM LETTER

The impersonal form letter is an objective way for the creditor to remind the debtor that he is overdue. By using a printed, computerized or Xeroxed form, the creditor tends to make the reminder quite impersonal.

Such a printed form usually consists of a statement of delinquency with blanks left to fill in as the creditor makes his routine request. For example:

Dear _____:

We would like to call your attention to the status of your account #_____ for _____ [date] amounting to $_____.

We hope it will have your immediate attention.

THE STAMPED REMINDER

The reminder note using a stamped notation on a copy of the original bill is a repetition of the notification stamp discussed earlier. The wording of such a stamp is similar to that shown in the notification section:

```
┌──────────────────────────┐
│       PAST DUE!          │
│  PLEASE REMIT TODAY!     │
└──────────────────────────┘
```

or

> **A FRIENDLY REMINDER:**
>
> **YOUR ACCOUNT IS OVERDUE.**
>
> **WE'RE EXPECTING A CHECK FROM YOU TODAY!**
>
> **WON'T YOU PLEASE OBLIGE?**

THE PRINTED FORM

There are printed stickers that can be applied to a copy of a bill to be sent out as reminders of overdue payments. These can be worded in all sorts of different ways:

> **WE MISSED YOUR PAYMENT FOR LAST MONTH. WON'T YOU PLEASE SEND IT TO US?**

or

> **YOUR ACCOUNT IS PAST DUE. WE'D LIKE TO HEAR FROM YOU—WITH A CHECK!**

USE OF THE PERSONAL LETTER

The personal letter is by and large the most versatile type of reminder letter the creditor can use to jog the memory of a debtor. The printed form and the printed reminder are limited to one use only. To send out a stamped bill for a second time merely repeats an unsuccessful action.

After using a printed form, a printed sticker or a stamped

reminder once, the creditor must come up with another means of attacking the problem. This can be done in the form of a planned series of reminder letters.

As it progresses, the series increases in urgency. The first is mild and courteous, excluding any implication of sharpness. The second becomes a bit more pointed. If a third letter is needed, it tends to be even more specific. Although politeness and courtesy are still evident in *all* reminder letters, the tone becomes a bit sharper and the request for money becomes definite and insistent.

Study this series of five:

> Dear Sir:
>
> Apparently you have overlooked your bill for $105 for the materials we sent you in October. It would be a great convenience to us to have your check as soon as possible.

> Dear Sir:
>
> May we again call your attention to the fact that you owe us $105 for the materials we sent you in October. You will be saved the additional bother of more reminders if you can send your remittance as soon as possible.

> Dear Sir:
>
> You have not communicated with us about the $105 you owe us for the materials we sent you during October. It is easy to misplace statements and overlook form notices. That's why we're sending this letter to remind you of your balance.
>
> The account is somewhat past due and we would appreciate your sending us a check in the next few days.

> Dear Sir:
>
> Have you overlooked the first payment on your account? The $105 you owe has been past due for two

months and is still unpaid. We wrote you regarding this matter in December, January and February. We have received no reply. We call your attention again to the need for settlement.

If there is any error or misunderstanding, will you please let us know immediately?

Dear Sir:

We again call your attention to your past-due account of $105. A detailed statement of the account has been mailed to you several times already. We would appreciate a remittance in settlement of this amount by return mail.

ANALYSIS OF THE REMINDER LETTER

The message central to the reminder letter is a routine and direct request. The creditor simply uses these communications to *remind* the debtor of the debt. The way to create a personal reminder letter is to present the problem as it exists—namely, the amount of money owed and the time it is overdue—and then move on to the request for action (in the upcoming stage).

The reminder phase is not a phase in which any special appeal is made to the debtor, nor is it a phase in which any conversation about the overdue debt is initiated.

Some advocates of collection methods even recommend humorous approaches in the reminder phase—short poems that are funny, anecdotes and even cartoons that relate to the creditor's business or services. If the amount of the bill is small, such a reminder can be effectively rendered in humor.

However, being in debt may strike the average person as being far from funny, particularly if the debtor is quite conscious of the lapsed bill and is struggling to do something about it.

The creditor must exercise good judgment and rely on an understanding of human nature in opting for humor or offbeat methods to remind a debtor of money owed.

One of the main things to remember about the reminder letter is that the basic assumption of the creditor is that the debtor has simply forgotten to pay the bill. The operative phrase that describes such an understanding might be "of course you know."

For example, in one of the first reminder letters, the creditor might write:

> Dear Mr. Brown:
> We have found in looking over our files that there is an outstanding charge of $250 against your account which is now past due. Of course you know that payment of our bills is due within thirty days of delivery.
> We'd like to determine when we can expect payment.

The phrase "of course you know" implies that the creditor's policy is known to the debtor. The word "when" in the final paragraph moves the situation one step closer to payment. The *assumed consent* now places the debtor in a position of not whether or not the bill will be paid, but *when*. To ignore or resist this psychological move is to admit the debtor has no intention of paying the money. It becomes a *commitment* to pay.

In the next few pages are a series of reminder letters which can be used in the first stage of the collection process—letters not involving discussion of payment, but based strictly on the psychological reminder of an unpaid debt.

This sample letter can be used first in a series of reminder letters:

> Dear Sir:
> It's a real pleasure to have you as a customer, and we want to do everything possible to serve you to the best of our ability.
> As you will recall when you opened your account, it was done with the understanding that you would

pay all of your bills promptly. That's why we were surprised to find that you have a balance that is now overdue.

We want nothing to spoil this pleasant relationship, and hope that you will send us a check right away to bring your account up to date.

This sample letter can be used after the first reminder letter in a series:

Dear Sir:

It's so easy to misfile or overlook a bill. We wonder if that is what happened to ours! We ask you because your account is approximately forty-five days overdue.

Please check our bill for $523 dated April 15 and forward your remittance unless you have some special reason for withholding payment. If you do, please let us know.

We look forward to receiving your reply or payment by return mail.

This sample letter can be number three in a series of reminder letters.

Dear Sir:

Perhaps you've forgotten that all of our bills are due and payable by the 10th of the month following the date of your purchase.

As we reminded you a short time ago, the unpaid balance shown on the last statement sent you has run considerably beyond this period.

Won't you please take a minute right now to make out a check, and drop it in the mail today?

Many thanks for your prompt cooperation.

Amount due: $532.

The sample letter can be used wherever needed in a sequence of reminder letters:

Dear Sir:

Have you been away?

If you have, we envy you—although we don't envy you the chore of wading through all the mail that has accumulated in your absence. Among those letters, you'll find a reminder that your account with us is past due.

Now that you are home, won't you please take a moment to send us a check for $532 so that your account will be up-to-date again?

Thank you.

Here is another sample that can be used at any time in the reminder sequence:

Dear Sir:

If you only knew . . .

- how hard it is to ask for money
- say just enough to get it
- without offending a good customer

. . . we are sure you would drop a check in the mail right away. So won't you please send us one today for the amount shown below?

Amount: $532.

Thank you?

Again, a sample that can be used in the reminder phase of the original "nudge" stage:

Dear Sir:

When the account of a good customer like you gets a little behind, we of course know there is bound to be a good, sound reason.

We are not in the least bit worried, but we would like to hear if there is anything wrong that we might be able to correct. Or, if there is any way that we could be helpful.

Should you have any questions about the charges

that make up your balance, please let us know and we'd be glad to send you this information. And may we say again what a pleasure it is to have you as a customer.

CHAPTER THIRTEEN

The Appeal:
Discussion Letters

Once it has been determined that reminder letters are not going to do any good, the collection process moves from stage one to stage two: The Appeal. This stage is also called the discussion stage, inasmuch as the purpose of the communications in the second stage is to effect a personal discussion about the debt and how to pay it off.

Depending on the type of customer, the type of account, and the general business situation, the first stage, The Nudge, usually consumes about thirty days between the moment the account becomes overdue to the moment at which it is determined that reminders are not going to initiate any action.

The second stage, The Appeal, occupies the lengthiest part of the collection process. It lasts from the thirtieth day to about the ninetieth day, although it may last much longer in certain instances.

After the second stage is finished, the collection process shifts briefly into the third stage, and then into the hands of a collection agency or of a lawyer, or into the small claims court.

ANATOMY OF THE APPEAL

The Appeal is a much more critical and complex stage than The Nudge. It differs from The Nudge in that the collection letters which make up its essential ingredient are based on a different assumption than the reminder letters.

In the reminder phase, as in the notification phase, the creditor assumes that the debtor has made an honest mistake and has simply overlooked the fact that the account is overdue. In the appeal stage, the creditor shifts his basic assumption from that of simple oversight to that of belief that something has gone wrong and that there is good reason to suspect that there will be further delay in settlement of the debt. (**Note:** Once The Nudge stage has passed, the creditor never again reverts to the assumption that the delay is caused by oversight.)

The underlying purpose of the appeal stage is to discover what is holding up the payment and then, in turn, to work out a payment plan (either for a part or the entire amount) with the debtor.

Because the process of sympathetic interrogation and then impersonal discussion is a difficult one, the appeal letter—or, actually, the series of appeal letters—must be carefully thought out ahead of time and must be cautiously written in order for the creditor to retain the debtor's confidence and good will while maintaining his determination to collect.

The importance of the discussion letter cannot be overstressed. Each communication must be a part of an ongoing series, building in intensity and aimed at a climax. The series can number from five to ten—depending on the creditor's wishes and his understanding of his relationship with his debtor. Discussion letters are sent out periodically until a meeting can be initiated.

At the point of discussion, each individual case becomes an entity in itself, to be handled on an individual basis. The purpose of the discussion letter is to initiate a dialogue; the dialogue itself can take the form of a number of different kinds of plans for settlement of the debt. (More about that later in this chapter.)

APPEALS USED IN THE DISCUSSION LETTER

The key element of the discussion letter is the specific appeal around which it is constructed. While the reminder letter simply keeps the fact of the unpaid account before the eyes of the debtor, the discussion letter tries to motivate the debtor to pay. The assumption, of course, is that the debtor has found it impossible to pay and does not know what to do. Emotional appeal is the element of the discussion letter which, it is hoped, will spur the debtor to action.

Most commonly used are appeals to sympathy, pride, justice, self-interest, cooperation and to fear. (**Note:** The appeal to fear should not be used in The Appeal, but in the next stage, The Push. It will be discussed in detail in the following chapter.)

THE APPEAL TO SYMPATHY

The use of the appeal to sympathy usually tries to make the debtor aware that the creditor has done him a favor by extending credit. Because of this favor, the creditor now finds himself very much inconvenienced, and perhaps even suffering as a result of the debtor's nonpayment. The debtor's sympathy is the target; if that sympathy is aroused enough, he will contact the creditor and try to work something out.

There are obvious faults and disadvantages to the use of this appeal. In less than skillful hands, the appeal becomes almost a whining and groveling plea for money. The average debtor cannot find much sympathy for a prosperous concern when his own status is a serious, debt-riddled one.

However, if the creditor can couch the appeal in believable terms, the appeal to sympathy can be a powerful one. The trick is for the creditor to know his debtor and to know how to appeal to his sympathy; or, if the debtor's sympathy may be suspect, to avoid that appeal completely.

> Dear Sir:
> Would you please help us keep costs down? By sending your check with the enclosed bill now, you help us avoid the expense of sending additional reminders and letters. That saves both postage and clerical expense . . . savings we can then pass on to you and our customers.

THE APPEAL TO PRIDE

The use of the appeal to pride is an attempt to make the debtor feel shame at being in debt. Pride and self-respect are important character traits in most people. It is only when it becomes impossible for the average person to pay his debts that he defaults—so goes the average belief.

To point out to a debtor how well he has paid his bills in the past and how pleasant the creditor has found it dealing with him is a powerful emotional appeal. In many cases the correctly worded appeal of this kind to pride and self-respect may turn the trick.

> Dear Sir:
> We could not help holding in high esteem the standards which you had for prompt payment of your account in the past. We want you to know that we have appreciated this.
> At the present time, however, your account is past due. . . .

THE APPEAL TO JUSTICE

The point of the appeal to justice is to try to make the debtor feel that he is not dealing fairly with the creditor. The stress is on the valuable service or product the creditor is responsible for, on the promptness of its delivery and on the creditor's businesslike dealings. It is not fair to the creditor that he be forced to wait any longer for his money.

In this appeal the creditor can sometimes even allow himself the indulgence to remonstrate briefly with the debtor.

> Dear Sir:
>
> We confidently expected a remittance on your account for $334 as a response to our last letter.
>
> Frankly, we were disappointed, for we cannot believe that you would intentionally impose on us. And that is really what it amounts to. By not remitting promptly, you do impose upon us the difficulties of carrying the account longer than we had agreed to do.
>
> You know the importance of prompt collections. We are still confident that we can count on you to be fair and just with us in this situation.

THE APPEAL TO SELF-INTEREST

The use of the appeal to self-interest can be a more potent appeal than those to sympathy and pride. A letter appealing to self-interest usually comes toward the end of the discussion letter series. Its tone is usually more insistent than those of the earlier appeals.

The use of logic and a slight undercurrent of threat can make for an effective and veiled warning—although the threat itself is never really exposed. The debtor must see that it is in his own best interests to pay his account immediately, otherwise his credit standing may be jeopardized. No indication is made that the creditor will take action regarding the debtor's credit standing, but the implication is there.

> Dear Sir:
>
> We have several times already called your attention to the unpaid balance of $125 on your account. Why have we heard nothing from you?
>
> In simple language, we are disappointed. When

111

you asked for credit, we felt warranted in placing
confidence in you. You have not done your share to
uphold our confidence.

It is unnecessary to point out to an astute businessperson like you that only by meeting obligations justly
can a firm maintain its credit standing in the community. You cannot afford to lose the good will of your
suppliers by allowing knowledge of your nonpayment
to circulate among the trade.

We hope that you will restore our original confidence with prompt payment. Put your check in the
mail today. Let's close this past chapter and start out
anew with a fresh slate.

A MIXTURE OF APPEALS

The creditor need not confine any discussion letter to only
one appeal, but can combine several. Here is a letter that uses
positive pride and self-interest plus a negative loss of comforts
and advantages appeal:

Dear Sir:

You and your wife made a wise decision when you
purchased your bedroom set from us last February.
No family can be comfortable without furniture that
is well-designed and sturdy.

So that you can continue to enjoy the comfort and
security of your home furnishings, it is important you
keep up your payments on these pieces. Four messages
have been mailed to you at thirty-day intervals: April
15, May 15, June 15, and July 15. You now owe $1050
for three payments that are past due.

It is easy to become so accustomed to the privilege
of credit that it is taken for granted. You were lucky
to buy when you did, for this month, the same set
would cost one-half again as much as you paid.

You'll agree that you can't afford to risk losing the

comforts and advantages of those pieces you now enjoy.

Please send your check for $1050 today or call me by telephone so we can discuss a satisfactory solution.

Note the appeal in paragraph one to general pride and self-satisfaction. Then, in paragraph two, the appeal to self-interest and family interests. Paragraphs three and four include an appeal to self-interest tempered with a slight threat of loss.

THE APPEAL FOR DISCUSSION

Toward the end of the appeal stage, at least one letter should be inserted in which the debtor is offered the opportunity to explain his nonpayment. In such a letter, the creditor can offer to sit down with the debtor to discuss a settlement of the issue.

Such an appeal may bring a positive response; it is an honest appeal and it may affect the debtor favorably. Then, during the discussion, the details may be worked out by creditor and debtor to the satisfaction of both.

The purpose of the discussion letter at the end of the appeal stage is to bring about a dialogue between creditor and debtor after the creditor has appealed as much as possible to the debtor's pride and self-interest. It is this discussion which is the target of the mounting intensity of the letter series in the appeal stage.

Once this dialogue is under way, the collection process moves into a brand new phase. It is still part of stage two, and it is still part of the collections routine, but the action has moved past reminders and pleas. It is now in a nuts-and-bolts situation.

The creditor is now able to advance a plan for settlement of the overdue account. There are several possibilities available for payment of the overdue debt—ways that make it easier for the debtor than up-front settlement for the entire amount owed. Among the possibilities are:

- Imminent settlement
- Extension of account
- Promissory note
- Postdated check
- Partial payment
- Negotiation.

IMMINENT SETTLEMENT

The best of all possible solutions to the discussion is an agreement for imminent or immediate settlement of the overdue account. However, since by its very nature the basic discussion phase usually assumes outright payment is unlikely, that outcome is rare.

EXTENSION OF ACCOUNT

A common means of arriving at a possible settlement is for the creditor to suggest an extension of the account, that is, a deferral of payment for another thirty days. The creditor must know the debtor very well in order to offer such a suggestion. Otherwise, the same thing may happen to the extension as happened to the original bill: the debtor may simply forget about it or ignore it.

Unless the debtor can offer proof of payment, or at least a satisfactory and reasonable explanation of why the debt was not paid on time in the first place, the creditor should refrain from offering any such extension.

PROMISSORY NOTE

An alternative to the extension of the account is the issuance of a promissory note for the full amount of the debt. The promissory note is simply a loan, on paper, of the amount owed, with appropriate interest added to the total amount.

The advantage of the promissory note is that it is made out with a third party—usually a bank—holding the note and acting as an authoritarian figure for future payment.

114

Besides, the creditor now has the money; the payment of the note is a transaction between the debtor and the bank.

POSTDATED CHECK

Another possibility is for the creditor to suggest that the debtor pay the bill with a postdated check. This solution usually involves a situation in which the debtor is without funds at the moment, but expects a substantial amount of cash in the very near future. Of course, the creditor must make sure the windfall is not simply a figment of the debtor's overactive imagination.

The advantage of the postdated check is that the creditor at least has the amount of money—potentially—in hand. If the check bounces, of course, the creditor is back on square one.

PARTIAL PAYMENT

One of the most common methods of achieving settlement is for the creditor to suggest a schedule of payment, breaking up the total debt into several parts.

For example, if the debtor owes $1000, the creditor may break that up into four payments of $250 each—one immediately and the balance paid in three monthly installments.

The creditor can choose to ignore any interest due, or he can charge it and add it to the final payment. However, with certain debtors and in certain situations, the addition of interest due at a fair rate is not unreasonable.

NEGOTIATION

Almost as common as the partial payment of the account is the possibility of negotiation. The debtor may bring up a question of quality or quantity of the goods or service provided by the creditor. This fact then calls for negotiation between creditor and debtor. If a bargain can be struck immediately, the

settlement may be reached in the first dialogue between creditor and debtor.

If, however, the problem is a bit knottier than one offering
a simple and immediate solution, the negotiations may continue
for some time. Usually creditor and debtor can reach an agreement without the use of a lawyer or the courts.

If not, the creditor must hire an attorney and use the court
system, or use the small claims court to try his case before an
arbitrator.

SAMPLE DISCUSSION LETTERS

In the next few pages are a series of letters urging discussion of the unpaid debt. These letters can be sent out one
after the other—usually after a series of appeal letters has
been tried.

The following letter is a retailer's first letter in a series:

> Dear Sir:
> Though you have neither paid the balance on your
> account, which is now long overdue, nor replied to
> any of our reminders, we are still reluctant to assume
> you would purposely ignore us.
> If you have a problem which we can help you with,
> you may expect, of course, our full cooperation. You
> must come in to see us, however, within the next five
> days or send us your check for the full amount due.
> Remember, too, that you save service charges by
> paying off what you owe.

Here is a follow-up to the first discussion letter:

> Dear Sir:
> We are sure you'll agree that it is always easier to
> "talk" over anything of a personal nature, rather than
> attempt to do it by mail.
> That is why we would appreciate your stopping in

to see us about your account. It's nothing serious, but we would like the opportunity of straightening out what is apparently a misunderstanding about our terms.

So will you please come in as soon as possible? Or, if it would be more convenient, just telephone me at the number on the letterhead.

May we hear from you soon?

The following is a fourth-month follow-up letter, containing a typical appeal to self-interest and pride:

Dear Sir:

You must be proud of your good credit standing here which enables you to buy *what* you want *when* you want it, on a convenient charge account basis.

We are delighted to make this easy, modern method of shopping available to you, and are anxious for you to continue enjoying this privilege. But you can surely appreciate that if we are to be of this service to you, it will be necessary for you to abide by our credit terms.

These state that all bills are due and payable thirty days following date of purchase.

So won't you please mail us a check for your overdue balance? Of, if you can't send us the full amount, then at least let us have a substantial payment on account right away.

Your prompt cooperation will be appreciated.

Here is a letter in which the intensity of the appeal is heightened and in which the veiled threat almost shows through:

Dear Sir:

To retain *your* good will is always our first consideration. That is the reason we are worried that you have not replied to any of our reminders that your account is now long overdue.

For when customers don't get in touch with us, we can only assume that they are not interested in keeping their account up-to-date. And obviously that means it might be necessary to restrict future purchases. We don't want that to happen, and we are sure you don't either.

So won't you please send us a check at once? Or come in to see us within the next five days.

The following letter combines an appeal to self-interest and a threat of cutting off credit with an appeal to come in to discuss the situation.

Dear Sir:

Have you ever stopped to consider how vitally important a good credit rating might be to you some day? Suppose there is something you need desperately for yourself or your loved ones, but you haven't the ready cash to buy it. That's where credit can mean so much to you and yours.

Now take that old amount you have owed us for so long on your account. We don't expect you to settle it all at once. But if you would only stop in and see us, we'll gladly work out some arrangement for paying it off that will fit your bank account.

So do get in touch with us this week. You'll find us most cooperative.

This letter stresses the importance of good credit, and at the same time asks the debtor to come in for a chat:

Dear Sir:

We don't expect you to settle it all at once. We mean that old bill you have owed us for quite some time. But if you will only stop in, we're sure some plan for paying it off can be worked out that will fit your budget, and thus protect your credit standing.

Perhaps you've never thought much about what

good credit can mean to you and your family. It's like the well that ran dry—something you may never miss until you have lost it.

Consider these points for example:

- Credit enables you to buy whatever you want when you want or need it, whether you have the ready cash or not.
- It allows you to budget out of income, instead of paying out large sums when is inconvenient to do so.
- It gives you financial standing, a critical factor when purchasing a home or car, or anything else of major importance.
- It saves you money, enabling you to buy when prices are the lowest at special sales.

We are sure you realize these things, and will not misunderstand our reason for pointing them out. You'll find us anxious to aid you in every way we can. So do come in soon and let's talk it over.

Your balance is $576.

CHAPTER FOURTEEN

The Push:
Urgency Letters

After the critical and complex emotional appeals and intellec-
tual persuasion evidenced in the letters of the appeal stage,
most delinquent clients will agree to a discussion with their
creditors. Once actual discussion is initiated, the collection
situation becomes a thing of the past.

However, for the one delinquent in a hundred, even the
most intense of appeals may not produce money. Whether the
reason is the debtor's actual inability to pay or his adamant
refusal to honor the debt, the situation moves on into stage
three, The Push. This stage is also called the "urgency" stage.

Now the creditor's assumption is simply that the debtor
cannot or will not pay his bill. Even so, the creditor still tries
to persuade the debtor to act. At the same time, he makes it
clear that he is about to put the matter of the unpaid account
in the hands of a collection agency or an attorney.

Basically, the creditor is using the most intense of all
appeals—fear—as the weapon.

THE APPEAL TO FEAR

Although there is the hidden appeal to fear in almost every appeal letter composed, an obvious appeal to fear should be reserved for a final letter in stage three. This letter, which immediately precedes a crucial move to force payment, underlines the seriousness of the debtor's position.

One method of appealing to fear is for the creditor to remind the debtor that he is required to report periodically all unpaid accounts to the retail merchant's association to which he belongs. The disadvantage of using fear as an appeal is the fact that such an appeal is only a hairline away from action, and is simply a last-ditch effort to force a move.

> Dear Sir:
> I would like to make a suggestion to you.
> At the next meeting of the Tilden County Retail Merchant's Association, your name will be reported among those who have been owing merchants hereabouts for a considerable length of time.
> This is only in line with the rules of the association. I have no choice in this matter.
> Would you like an opportunity to prevent this action? If so, simply pay the $523 which you now owe us. If satisfactory arrangements are made by June 3, your name will not be reported.
> We hope you will act promptly to clear up your account with us. That will be the much better thing for you in all ways.

SERIOUS AND CRITICAL ACTION

If he has not done so in the preliminary stages of collection, in stage three the creditor now takes personal control of the collection process. During The Push the matter has moved beyond the stage of appeal and is now only a step away from serious and critical action.

Even so, the creditor always leaves a loophole for the debtor, if, even at this late date, he decides to pay up the account. However, the underlying tone of The Push letter is one of seriousness. The appeal is directly to fear, although the creditor is usually careful not to make an open threat.

The typical letter may focus on three main facets of the problem:

- A view of the situation from the beginning, with total objectivity.
- The decision to turn the affair over into the hands of a professional collector. (The appeal here is to fear.)
- The loophole or last plea. (The appeal here is to self-interest and pride.)

The stage of urgency does not need to be closed off with one final letter. There might be two or three, each stressing the coming action, but never setting the date until the final letter. Once the date for the action is set, there can be no follow-up communications.

LETTERS IN THE URGENCY STAGE

A typical opening letter for The Push might go like this:

Dear Sir:

The time has finally come when we are forced to write the kind of letter that we dislike writing very much. You have been asked time and time again in our previous letters to pay up your long-overdue bill, which is now $790. We have done everything we can to persuade you to do so. Unfortunately, we have received no replies to our many requests.

Do we have to resort to the only move we have left, namely, to turn your account over to an attorney for collection? A lawsuit is always an unfortunate ending to any relationship. You will be required to pay not only the bill, but also court costs. We do not want to take this step without giving you at least one last chance to write us and to let us know your side of the story.

We have done business together for many years. It's a sad thought that this friendship must end in this unfortunate and unpleasant way. Please write to us immediately—or, better still, send us your check to pay this debt, now ninety days past due. But do it today, please.

Such a letter can stand as the first one in a series of personal appeals. The creditor can also use the same form if he wishes to close out the problem with just one letter by simply adding this paragraph:

We will delay action on your account for five days— until September 5—before turning it over to our law firm.

Alternatively, if the creditor decides to use only one letter during The Push, he may take over the writing of the letter himself, rather than delegate it to the accounting department:

Dear Sir:

Your account has just been referred to me, marked for "final action."

Our policy is to keep all our contacts with our customers on a courteous and pleasant level. Therefore I am writing you this letter as a last resort. Will you please mail us your check for $235, or call personally to see me? I have deliberately withheld any action on your account and feel sure we can work out some mutually satisfactory arrangement for the settlement of your long-standing debt.

In the hopes that you will attend to this matter at once, I shall hold your account on my desk for ten days. Unless I hear from you by December 15, I shall have no alternative but to assign your account for collection. Hopefully, I anticipate that you will not force me to take such a step. It would have serious consequences upon your credit reputation.

THE USE OF A DRAFT ON A BANK

If the creditor is dealing with a debtor in a business enterprise in which the use of a draft on a bank is possible, it is during The Push that the creditor can make use of this expedient. (**Note:** Not all creditors can make use of the draft. Certain banks do not permit such drafts. For the businessperson not involved in a mercantile situation, the draft is rarely used.)

The action is explained in a letter just prior to the issuance of the draft:

Dear Sir:

Your account is now ninety days overdue, as we have pointed out in several letters.

This is as long as we feel we can carry the account, and unless we hear from you by November 5—five days from now—we assume that we have your permission to draw a draft on you for this amount. It will be drawn through the State National Bank.

We hope that you will avoid this inconvenient and roundabout method of paying, and at the same time prevent the unfavorable reflection on your credit standing at the bank, by remitting to us directly before the date indicated.

Let us hear from you by return mail.

TELEGRAM AND MAILGRAM MESSAGES

An alternative to a series of personal letters in The Push is the use of a telegram or mailgram. Such a mailgram message

124

is basically composed in the same fashion as a letter.
For example, the first in the series might say:

> YOUR ACCOUNT WILL BE REFERRED TO AN OUTSIDE
> COLLECTION AGENCY. ONLY YOUR REMITTANCE OF
> $720 WILL STOP FORMAL CREDIT ACTION. SEND IT
> TODAY.

Note in the above that the date has not been set for the final
action of moving the account into the hands of a collector or
attorney.
An alternate telegram might say:

> IMPORTANT YOU CALL COLLECT IMMEDIATELY
> BETWEEN 9A.M. AND 5P.M. CENTRAL STANDARD TIME
> CONCERNING YOUR CREDIT-CARD ACCOUNT. PLEASE
> TELL THE OPERATOR YOU RECEIVED THIS MESSAGE.

THE MISTAKE OF BECOMING ANGRY IN PRINT

The main concern in phrasing the urgency letter in The
Push is to keep it in mind that the customer may still be a
customer after the account is settled. It is necessary to consider
keeping his good will, no matter what is written.
It is inexcusable to display anger, allow harassing remarks,
or indulge in preaching to the debtor about paying his debts.
The line between simple invective and defamation is a thin
one. In letters of this sort, it is mandatory to:

- Make sure all the facts are scrupulously correct
- Use no malicious or defamatory accusations
- Indulge in no profanity or angry epithets
- Address the letter to the debtor personally in a
  sealed envelope
- Give the debtor at least one loophole in all letters.

Even the letter below contains a loophole:

125

Dear Sir:

The attached statement shows a part-due balance of $360 on your account. All our requests for payment have been unanswered.

Because our requests for payment have been ignored, we must assume that you don't have any questions or problems on the amount. Therefore, we must request immediate payment.

If our check isn't received on or before Thursday, April 9, we will find it necessary to turn your account over to our collection agency's representative.

To avoid this action, please send your check by return mail, using the attached self-addressed envelope.

Although the letter is worded as a final letter threatening to place an account with a collection agency, it is still possible for the creditor to telephone the debtor to find out what he is going to do and make some kind of arrangement for a discussion or for a disposition of the debt.

COLLECTION BY SPECIAL APPEALS

By the time the creditor has arrived at the final elements of stage three, it is sometimes possible to change tactics and make an appeal in a very special manner. If the collection process thus far has been straight-forward and objective, there is no real reason why the creditor can't resort to humor at the last moment.

Fresh, novel approaches have been useful in many instances, and their success has been a pleasant surprise to those who have tried to use it.

An appeal for money couched in humor must be very carefully composed. If forced, sarcastic, offensive or clumsy in any way—and, particularly if it is not written in the proper tone—its effectiveness will be lost.

The key element of good humor is its incongruity and its

surprising turn of thought in the midst of a long string of serious appeals. Originality is essential; stock humor can be adapted to new situations, but the effectiveness of an unusual appeal can be destroyed by using a method that is worn-out.

IT TAKES A SENSE OF THE ABSURD

The humorous collection letter is the most difficult of all for the average writer to compose. Humor is a very tricky bit of communications magic. It is least effective when used without skill and good judgment.

> Dear Sir:
> A collection letter always reminds me of a proposal of marriage. Take the young man. He hems and haws around all evening with the girl of his choice, when actually what he really wants to say is, "Will you marry me?"
> A credit manager acts the same way. He tries to think up all sorts of novel approaches, and appeals, when all he is trying to say is, "Will you send us a check?"
> So, without further ado, will you please? The amount is $77.

That letter, incidentally, proved 67 percent effective in bringing in money from delinquent customers.

One credit manager made it a habit to wind up his collection process just before sending out his final action letter with this communication:

> Dear Sir:
>
> PLEASE!
>
> Very truly yours. . . .

127

CHAPTER FIFTEEN

The Squeeze I: Small Claims Court

For the small business owner, professional or individual proprietor involved in an attempt to collect an overdue bill for a sum of less than $1000, the small claims court is a natural avenue of approach to a settlement.

However, this move, like the decision to hire an attorney or turn the account over to a collection agency, should occur only after the creditor has exhausted all standard means of collecting the bill.

Even though the creditor does not have to employ an attorney to appear for him in small claims court, he does have to pay several fees that reduce the amount of the debt collected.

Also, appearance in any court, including small claims court, takes time out of the creditor's business hours. Nevertheless, if the creditor's established collection plan fails to bring in the overdue money, the use of the small claims court can sometimes convince the debtor of the seriousness of the matter.

THE SMALL CLAIMS COURT

Today there are thousands of small claims courts in the United States. They hear over 3,500,000 cases each year, an increase of 25 percent in the past fifteen years. Although most small claims courts once handled only cases of less than $300, inflation has increased the maximum to about $1000 on the average, with at least $1500 in certain states (i.e., New York). An average maximum is now $750.

In many localities, an entity called "Small Claims Court" does not exist. Courts with this function and purpose are often called "magistrate's court." A quick look at the telephone listings and a call to town hall or city hall should resolve any questions you might have.

The creditor's advantage in dealing with the debtor in a small claims court is the speed and ease with which the case is handled. The presentation of the case usually takes only a few minutes. In most such courts, a supervisory judge will delegate the cases to a lawyer acting as arbitrator, unless the plaintiff insists on the judge's ruling. All but 10 percent of small claims cases are now decided by arbitrators appointed by the court.

The good news is that an arbitrator tends to judge a case not on the legal niceties and complications of the situation, but on simple equity and fairness.

WHO CAN FILE A SMALL CLAIM

Most state laws allow a creditor to sue a debtor for collection of money owed, either for a business debt or for a personal debt. However, a number of states prevent collection agencies or third parties to the debt from suing in these courts. In most cases the creditor can always bring suit by filing papers without the assistance of any third party.

STATUTE OF LIMITATIONS

Although laws vary from state to state, there is a statute of limitations on suing for nonpayment of debt. The limitation usually extends for four years from the day the contract was broken, that is, the day the bill becomes overdue.

However, while four years sounds like a great deal of time, it is always good advice for any creditor to begin suit as soon as possible after exhausting normal collection procedures. There are several reasons for moving quickly, which have nothing to do with the statute of limitations:

- Judges are notoriously less sympathetic to old claims than to new ones. The rationale is that the creditor doesn't particularly *want* to settle a claim if he lets it lapse for such a long time.

- Also, if a debtor is badly in arrears, it is better for the creditor to be at least at the head of the line waiting for payment if the debtor goes under and must liquidate his assets to pay off his debts.

HOW TO FILE IN SMALL CLAIMS COURT

Going to small claims court involves a number of very simple steps:

- Paying the filing fee
- Filing the plaintiff's statement
- Serving the plaintiff's claim
- Supplying documentary evidence
- Getting a hearing date.

PAYING THE FILING FEE

The fee in small claims court is usually a nominal one—usually $5 or $10, hardly ever over $10. However, the filing fee is only the first charge. In the case of a creditor who seeks money from a debtor, the procedure usually involves serving papers on the debtor to get him into court. The creditor may have to hire the services of a process server to accomplish this; that normally costs between $10 and $20. However, if the creditor wins the case, he can add filing fees and service costs to the court judgment.

FILING THE PLAINTIFF'S STATEMENT

All courts differ, requiring varying forms and papers. The creditor, who now becomes the *plaintiff*, fills out the *plaintiff's statement*. (The plaintiff's statement in small jurisdictions is called a *general claim* or a *plaintiff's claim*.) Essentially, the statement names the creditor, the debtor, the amount of the debt, the date of the debt, plus other pertinent details.

In turn, this handwritten form is typed up by the court clerk, and becomes the *claim of the plaintiff*. The creditor then signs the typewritten form; one copy of it goes to the judge; a second copy goes to the debtor, now called the *defendant*.

SERVING THE PLAINTIFF'S CLAIM

Depending on the rules of the local court, the debtor is now served with a summons to appear in small claims court. The claim against him is described in the plaintiff's statement. If the debtor is not available to be served with the papers, he must be tracked down. The creditor may have to pay a process server to find him.

There are several different ways for the creditor to serve papers on the debtor, including personal service, certified or registered mail and substituted service.

Personal service includes the use of a sheriff, marshal or constable—or a *disinterested adult*, a third party of age who is completely uninvolved in the case. The creditor can use the appropriate law officer to serve court papers on the debtor, with a cost of from $10 to $20. Some states have professional process servers; they can be found in the Yellow Pages.

The claim of plaintiff or notice of claim must be handed to the defendant personally. The server can't leave the paper in the mailbox or on the doorstep. The server must also make sure it is the debtor being served. If the debtor refuses to take the paper, acts hostile or runs off, the process server should put down the paper and leave. Valid service has been accomplished. The process server should never try to use force to get a defendant to take papers.

Certified or registered mail can be used to serve papers in most states. Normally, the court clerk mails the papers for the creditor, charging a small fee. This method of serving papers is an easy one, but the defendant (debtor) must be available to sign for the letter; his signature is proof of service. A debtor wise to the ways of evading servers will probably refuse to sign.

The creditor must find out from the clerk of the court whether or not the service of the process has been completed before the trial comes up.

Substituted service is also called nail-and-mail service. This type of service involves tacking one copy of the papers to the door and sending a similar copy through the mail to the person to be served, provided he can't be found. This method is usually used only when the debtor is adept at avoiding process servers and makes himself scarce. Certain states have complex laws involving this third method of serving papers; the creditor must work within his own state's system after learning its special rules.

Once the proper papers have been served, the creditor files a proof of service with the court clerk to let the court know that the debtor has been summoned to court.

SUPPLYING DOCUMENTARY EVIDENCE

In most cases, the creditor will not be required to show any papers to prove his case. However, if such papers are available, he should gather them together and show them to the clerk. If the clerk does not want to see them, the creditor can put them in a file for use during court appearance.

GETTING A HEARING DATE

A chief advantage of the small claims court is the speed with which cases are heard. Usually the creditor can set a court date when he files his papers. He should make sure he has allowed time for the papers to be served on the debtor. Most small claims courts are held during working hours on working days; some hold court in the evenings and on Saturdays.

THE CREDITOR'S DAY IN COURT

Appearing in a small claims court is quite different from appearing in a formal court. The creditor, the debtor and the arbitrator may be sitting at a small table in a crowded room, very close to one another. No one else will be listening to them as they talk. Nevertheless, the fact that the debtor has been brought to court tends to make him more likely to pay his debt.

The best way to prepare a case is to write down a very brief summation which will contain all the facts, stating the problem exactly. It is always preferable to back up such a statement with documents. A ledger sheet or a letter may be sufficient. If an informal contract has been written down before the transaction, the creditor should bring that along for evidence.

Oral contracts present a slight problem. However, the creditor can refer to people who may have been witness to the goods supplied or to the service rendered. A third person who has overheard a conversation between the creditor and the debtor about the nonpayment of the debt can attest to the fact of the debt.

The general atmosphere of a small claims court is much more relaxed than that of a regular court. The arbitrator will frequently ask questions. There is little to inject legal formalities or refuse to hear certain information because of a technicality, unless it is, of course, irrelevant. Ideally, the creditor should present his case as rapidly and as succinctly as he can, and then let the arbitrator take over.

WHAT IF THE DEBTOR DOESN'T SHOW UP?

Since the main problem in trying to collect debts is the fact that the debtor has failed to answer letters, phone calls and

even invitations to sit down for discussion, it is possible that
he may not show up for the court proceedings. In that case,
the creditor is awarded the judgment. In legal terms, such a
judgment is called a *default judgment,* that is, the plaintiff
has won the case by the default of the defendant.

It seems at first glance as if the creditor is now right back
in the same position he was before appearing in court. Such is
not actually the case. He now has the power of the court
behind him. Although he must go through several steps before
getting his money, he is in a favored position. The debt is now
on record, and the creditor has a court judgment in his favor.
He can do things now he could not do before.

HOW TO COLLECT A JUDGMENT AWARD

Open to the creditor with a court judgment are a number of
possibilities for settling his accounts. The money to cover the
judgment can legally be taken in several different places:

- Debtor's wages
- Debtor's bank account
- Debtor's motor vehicles
- Real property other than residence
- Receipts from debtor's business

Once the creditor knows something about the debtor—where
he works, where he runs his business, where he has his bank
account, where he keeps his motor vehicles and whether and
where he has real property other than his residence—then he
can proceed against him to seize enough to make up his
judgment.

FILING THE WRIT OF EXECUTION

Before he can proceed to levy on the debtor's wages or
other property, the creditor needs to obtain a court order

called a *Writ of Execution*. The way to get a writ of execution is to first of all obtain a small claims court judgment. Once the judgment is secured, the creditor files an application for the writ. The clerk will help the creditor fill it out; there is a small charge, recoverable later.

The creditor then sends the writ to the sheriff, marshal or proper law officer in the county where the debtor's assets are located. The creditor pays the law officer the proper fees for collection. He then gives him instructions on where to search and what to seize or collect.

To levy on a debtor's wages or bank account, the creditor needs the original and one copy of the writ of execution and a letter of instruction explaining what to do; i.e., "levy on the wages of . . .," "levy on the bank account of . . .," etc.

If the debtor has no job or bank account, the creditor can seize his motor vehicles—including cars, airplanes, boats, recreation vehicles and so on. This is more difficult than getting cash through a levy on wages or bank account. Usually a portion of the equity of a car is exempt from levy. Also a debtor's car could be in the name of another person. This method of paying off a judgment is extremely difficult, and often frustrating and complex.

It is even more difficult to obtain money through seizure of real property. The property must be seized, then put up for sale and money collected. A shortcut for the creditor is to prepare an abstract of judgment, file it in the county recorder's office and slap a lien against the property. Although this is essentially a nuisance action, it does mean that the debtor cannot sell the property without paying off the lien first. The creditor will eventually get his money.

As for other personal property—furniture and appliances— it usually isn't worth the trouble to levy on them, because they are probably covered by state exemption laws.

For the record, a levy on the debtor's salary or wages is known legally as *garnishment;* the act of levying on wages is called *garnisheeing* them. Most states have limits on the amount of money from each pay check that can be taken, either as a specific limit of the amount, or a percentage of the take-home

135

wages. For a fuller discussion, see Chapter Seventeen.

The levy on a debtor's bank account is called *attachment*. Certain laws also cover the amount to be attached. In fact, the levy on property is also called attachment; again, laws limit the amount that can be taken. (See Chapter Seventeen.)

SEIZING THE DEBTOR'S BUSINESS ASSETS

Statutes differ from state to state, but the creditor can usually hire an officer of the law to intercept ready cash that comes into the hands of the debtor, if he is in business for himself.

One form of this type of collection is the so-called till tap. The law officer picks up all the money in the cash register at the time he visits the business. These collections are continued until the judgment is satisfied. The fee for such a service usually costs $10 to $35

Another method of intercepting money is the *eight-hour keeper*. The officer remains at the place of business all day and collects every cent of the money that comes in. For this service he usually charges from $35 to $70.

A third method is the *two-day keeper*. The officer stays at the business during working hours for a period of two days and collects what comes in. The average fee for this service is from $200 to $350.

ADVANTAGES OF SUING THROUGH SMALL CLAIMS

Although many creditors prefer to work through collection agencies and attorneys, the use of the small claims court has an advantage with its simple operation and speed of action. Also, the costs are considerably lower than the costs of a collection agency and an attorney.

With the backing of the small claims court, the creditor can do almost as much by himself as an attorney or a collection agent can—particularly when it comes to attaching the debtor's wages (garnisheeing them), seizing his bank account (attaching it) or obtaining money from the sale of his vehicles.

DOS AND DON'TS FOR THE CREDITOR IN SMALL CLAIMS COURT

Here are a few tips and suggestions for the creditor who takes a debtor to small claims court:

- Be prepared to wait at least two weeks for the case to come up.
- Make sure to show up for the trial on time, although you may have to wait once you get there.
- Don't be surprised if small claims court is only open on weekends or during the evening.
- Bring all papers, bills, and other items to help you prove your case.
- Prepare to have witnesses if they are necessary to help your case.
- Be prepared to spend some time at the court once you get there.
- State your case as succinctly and clearly as possible.
- Avoid long-winded explanations at all times.
- Keep a firm rein on your temper.
- Never descend to vituperation, slander, or obscenity.

CHAPTER SIXTEEN

The Squeeze II:
The Collection Agency

For the busy professional, individual proprietor or business-person, small claims court may prove unfeasible because of the amount of the claim or because of the time involved away from work. The creditor's next move, once he has exhausted all possible means of bringing a debtor to heel without success, may be to turn the matter over to a professional collection agency or agent.

However, placing an account in the hands of a professional collection agency will likely disrupt the relationship between creditor and debtor permanently. This move is irrevocable and should not be taken lightly. (**Note:** Once the creditor has surrendered the collection problem to a professional agency, he must remain out of the picture until some result is obtained by the agency. The creditor should have nothing more to do with trying to collect the debt.)

Professional bill collectors can sometimes apply more pressure to the debtor than can the creditor. There is sometimes a personal relationship between creditor and debtor that may stand in the way of settlement.

The third-party agent begins his process by writing one or more letters to the debtor, urging him in strong terms to make payment and pointing out the unpleasant consequences in not doing so. Usually a member of the collection agency then makes a call on the debtor to present the demands in person. Although the agent's methods may be similar to those of the creditor, in most cases the pressure exerted is taken more seriously.

CHOOSING THE RIGHT COLLECTION AGENCY

Most creditors not using the small claims court choose a collection agency over an attorney because the agency tends to be more systematic in following up accounts. A collection agency also has a standard series of letters ready to send before being forced in turn to give the account to their own attorney.

There are about 5000 collection agencies operating now in the United States; their methods and success differs markedly. The creditor is faced with the unenviable problem of trying to choose the right one. Before making a choice, the creditor should make sure the agency has an office in the area where the debtor is located.

The most important point in trying to select the proper agency is to pick out the one that has a good reputation and is not known for ruthless or irresponsible acts. One thing the creditor should watch out for is the use of misrepresentative names—"federal," "national," "United States," "Bureau of Records" and "Department of Credit"—in the titles of the agencies.

THE FREE-DEMAND SERVICE

The collection agency chosen should operate a *free-demand service*. This means that the creditor prepares a form in triplicate, sends one copy to the debtor, the second to the agency and the third to his file. The original copy states in so many words that if payment isn't received, the agency will take "any steps necessary" to get the money.

If, at the end of a specified time, usually ten days, there isn't any action, the agency then gets to work. If, within that interim ten days, the creditor receives the money, he must notify the agency immediately so that no further effort will be made to collect it.

In some cases the bill will be paid up during this ten days—the free-demand service time—and the creditor needs to pay the agency nothing!

However, if the creditor feels that the debtor will *not* pay up in that ten-day period, he should institute the *regular collection service*, in which he sends a notice of the debt and its history only to the agency, and ignores the debtor. The agency then starts action *immediately*.

HOW MUCH DOES IT COST?

Fees and rates charged by collection agencies vary throughout the country, but are usually fairly uniform within several percentage points. Most of them charge according to the fees set up originally by the Commercial Law League of America. These rates run as follows:

- Fifteen percent on the first $750 collected
- Ten percent on the excess of $750 collected
- Minimum charge of $15
- On items of $45 or less, 33⅓ percent.

On the other hand, no collection agency or attorney is absolutely bound to charge only that much. A general survey on collection agencies—called "corporate knee-breakers" in a recent issue of *Time* magazine—claimed that most of them "skimmed" from 20 percent to 25 percent off the top of each collected debt.

"Be sure to settle the matter of fees before you place the account," says Donald R. Kitzing, in a recent book on credit and collections. Most reputable collection agencies have regular fee schedules which are sent to the client—the creditor—when first contacted.

THE ADDITION OF ATTORNEY'S FEES

When the collection agency is forced to give up its actions and turn the account over to an attorney, the fee goes up. The agency might charge 6 percent more on the first $750, 5 percent more on the next $750 and 3 percent more on the excess. This, in turn, helps the agency pay off the attorney.

In the retail field, the fees are generally higher: 25 percent for all accounts that are settled with personal calls or litigation; up to 33 and 50 percent for all other accounts! When an account is forwarded by the agency to an attorney, the practice is for the agency to retain one-third of the fee and to give two-thirds to the attorney.

The creditor must know the amount of the fee before he instructs the collection agency to proceed with the case.

When an agency is forced to turn the account over to an attorney, the creditor will be informed of the move and will be apprised of the amount of the additional fee, if any. Some agents do not charge extra; others do.

HOW THE COLLECTION AGENCY WORKS

The collection agency may not be able to recover the total amount of the lapsed account. It may offer a partial settlement of the debt, say 25, 50 or 75 percent. The agency may recommend that the creditor agree to such a settlement. The final decision is always up to the creditor. However, many factors may be at issue in making such a decision.

In a partial settlement, the deadbeat tends to win out. Let's assume that the debtor owes $1000 to a creditor. Up to the time of settlement, he has not paid one red cent to the creditor. By that time, the creditor already owes the agency between 15 and 20 percent of the hypothetical $1000.

If the deadbeat agrees to settle for $500, and assuming the fee is 20 percent, the creditor must pay the agency $100. He gets only $400 for all his grief and pains. Paying 40 percent of an honest debt is a disgraceful way to do business, and can be a disaster for the creditor.

Perhaps the debtor is not a deadbeat, but a sorely pressed businessperson. In that case, assuming that the creditor wants to do business with him again, he should hold out for full settlement. The fee to the agency can be laid off to costs and the status quo retained.

However, by the time a creditor hands over an unpaid account to a collection agency, the relationship is usually destroyed for good. Certainly, if the debtor manages to pay only 40 percent of the claim, the creditor is a fool ever to deal with him again.

A TYPICAL SETTLEMENT OF A CLAIM

One collection agency that has eighty-five branches around the world is the Financial Collection Agencies of Malden, Massachusetts. The agency's manager, Gary Golditch, once told a magazine writer how he tried to make his debtors pay up.

The most important point to keep in mind, he said, was never to let the debtor hang up once he was reached by telephone. Golditch's method is to start out being completely polite and ingratiating.

"I'm sorry to inconvenience you, but you owe a bill of $450 to my client."

Then, when the facts have been detailed, Golditch moves on to stress the point of moral responsibility. "You received the merchandise you wanted, but my client has not been paid yet. It is now over three months in arrears."

From that point on, Golditch simply relies on his own instincts of persuasion to try to convince the debtor that he should pay up the overdue account.

Quite soon he advances his own "payment plan." "I've looked up your financial situation, and I believe your best method of paying up would be to take out a new credit-card loan, or perhaps execute a cosigned bank note."

Golditch and his company recover about one-fifth of all the overdue accounts they try to collect on. He feels that saddling a debtor with another debt in order to pay off one is not a good way to get out of debt. He never advises anyone to do so when the debtor can't handle it.

"I have a moral commitment to work out an equitable agreement," he says.

CHAPTER SEVENTEEN

The Squeeze III: The Attorney

For one reason or another, the small businessperson, professional or individual proprietor may want to bypass the use of the small claims court and collection agency and hand over the unpaid account to an attorney. A claim levied against an individual rather than a company—the kind of account the average professional might encounter—may not be handled by all collection agencies.

If the creditor has gone through all the motions and exhausted his own collection procedures, he still has a number of "rights and remedies"—in the legal sense—that he can resort to through an attorney. They include such legal moves as: litigation, attachment, garnishment and lien.

Each of these resources involves the action of the court, and requires the services of an attorney. Nevertheless, a creditor must be aware of these several avenues through which he can try to approach a solution to an overdue account. (Note: Generally, most rights and remedies open to the creditor involve statutes that are of a local, not federal, nature. Most of these exist on a state or county level. Because of their very nature, they are individual and unlike similar statutes in adjoining stages—at least in their all-important details and conditions. For that reason, most of the discussion here is limited to points of a *general* nature. It is up to the creditor to explore the details of his own local legal machinery for the specifics of his own situation.)

THE RIGHT OF LITIGATION

Any creditor has the right to go to court to force a debtor to pay up an overdue debt. By working through an attorney, the creditor can usually exert a great deal more pressure than he can through his own devices. The attorney, like his client, goes through a series of prescribed steps in trying to collect the money.

First of all, he writes several letters, and if no money is forthcoming, he finally tells the debtor that he is going to take him to court. If that fails to elicit any response, the attorney, with the knowledge of the creditor, takes the debtor to court to obtain the money through court action. Beware! (It is *extremely* expensive to collect money through formal court channels. In many cases, the creditor must pay fees and charges that may in the long run cost him more than the amount of the unpaid account.)

There are both advantages and disadvantages in using the regular courts to collect. However, if the situation finally becomes insoluble and a lawsuit is instituted, the creditor must ascertain several crucial facts about the debtor and his situation before bringing suit.

Most important of all, he must determine whether or not the debtor possesses unencumbered property on which to levy, in order to secure a judgment. Either that, or the creditor must determine if the debtor has income enough to make garnishment proceedings feasible.

A rule of thumb by which a creditor can determine the feasibility of attaching through garnishment or attachment is as follows: The debtor must own property valued at least in the amount of the claim plus the expenses involved in the suit. The creditor can get this information in most cases either from the attorney or the collection agency. If no such property or viable income exists, the creditor should never undertake to bring suit. It is pointless, as the old saying goes, to try to squeeze blood out of a turnip.

USING AN ATTORNEY TO COLLECT MONEY

Obtaining money owed through the courts is a complicated procedure. The case usually consists of three separate stages of action:

- Pleading the case
- Trying the case
- Executing the settlement.

PLEADING THE CASE

In the first stage, the creditor is represented as plaintiff by his attorney. The attorney establishes the fact and terms of the exchange or service, files a petition and asks for the service of a summons upon the debtor (defendant). After the process is served, the debtor can file an answer, setting up a defense. If there is no answer, a default judgment results.

TRYING THE CASE

The second stage consists of the trial. The judge renders a verdict either for the plaintiff (creditor) or the defendant (debtor). If in favor of the plaintiff, a court decree determines the amount due from the defendant. In some states, the judgment automatically becomes a lien upon the defendant's real estate and personal property at this point in the proceedings.

EXECUTING THE SETTLEMENT

Execution of judgment, an order of the court directing the sheriff, bailiff, marshal, constable or officer of the court to collect the amount of the judgment out of the property of the debtor, follows. The officer seizes the property and advertises it for sale at public auction. The proceeds are turned over to the court, the court fees are taken out of the amount and the creditor winds up with what is left. If no property is available for seizure, the judgment is "docketed" for future use if and when the debtor acquires property.

If the sum to be recovered is less than $1000, it pays the creditor to make use of the small claims court. (See Chapter Fifteen.) The process is less complex, and the creditor himself acts in his own behalf without the services of a lawyer. The only drawback is that the small claims court has no ability to enforce payment and the creditor must go about it himself.

THE RIGHT OF ATTACHMENT

One obvious move for a person to make when he is deeply in debt but does not have the ready cash to pay off his accounts is to borrow and pay off his bills before starting up in business again. However, for the less honorable debtor, the most obvious move is to sell all his holdings quickly, convert them into cash and stash the money away in a far-off bank—and laugh at his creditors.

Attachment is a legal provision through which the debtor's property can be seized and taken out of his control to be held for payment of debts on which suit has been brought in court by his creditor. Attachment can also be made prior to bringing suit, but usually the case must be brought into court within thirty days of the time the attachment writ is served.

The purpose of attachment is to prevent debtors who are wealthy with plenty of resources at their command from welching on their debts and providing themselves with the ability to convert their properties to money which they deposit in some far-off bank where it cannot be touched by the creditor.

The right of attachment is available in almost all courts in the land, although the details of each statute differs. The typical attachment proceeding is a highly technical and complex one. All local requirements must be strictly adhered to for the proper execution of the process.

Generally speaking, however, the reasons for seeking attachment are usually the same in most states:

- The debtor is hiding out with the intent of defrauding creditors or to avoid the service of legal processes.
- The debtor has left the state with the intent of defrauding creditors or to avoid the service of legal processes.
- The debtor has removed property or is about to dispose of property for the purpose of defrauding his creditors.

The most obvious grounds for seeking attachment are that an element of fraud or concealment, or removal of property from the jurisdiction exists and can be proved at the time of the issuance of the attachment writ.

PROPER PROCEDURE FOR ATTACHMENT

The creditor is usually required to make an affidavit stating the amount of the debt; stating that the claim is just and that no part of the debt has been paid; giving the history of the indebtedness; stating that the creditor does not owe money to the debtor and that the sum demanded is due; and stating the reason (grounds) for the attachment. The creditor sometimes can make the affidavit, and sometimes an attorney or agent is required.

In most states the creditor is also required to give a bond to protect the debtor against injuries resulting from a wrongful attachment.

Once the writ is issued, an officer of the court proceeds to attach enough property to satisfy the creditor's claim, together with costs and expenses. On the day specified in the writ, the officer of the court reports on the procedure. The attachment then becomes a lien, or hold, on the debtor's property. This lien is later made absolute by judgment.

An attachment is dissolved and the property released when the debtor tenders a bond for the payment of whatever judgment is rendered against him, usually in the same amount.

THE RIGHT OF GARNISHMENT

When a debtor does not have sufficient property to provide money enough to pay off an unpaid account, the creditor can acquire a lien or right to take possession of money owned him by any third party. Usually that third party is an employer who pays the debtor a salary. The employer, in legal terms, becomes the *garnishee,* and the money held by lien the *garnishment.*

The employer, or third person who owes money to the debtor, is a completely innocent party in this legal action. He becomes legally the *trustee or custodian* of the property or debt. The court action is a restraint on him to prevent payment of his debt or obligation, in effect diverting that money to the original creditor.

What happens is that the court informs the garnishee (employer) that he is not to settle with the defendant (debtor), but to answer the suit of the plaintiff (creditor).

This sounds quite complicated, but most statutes provide for such an interception of money to pay off a creditor's lien on a certain amount. In some states, garnisheeing money is called a *trustee process,* a *judgment execution* or simply an *attachment.* The details of garnishment in various states differ in many elements. The creditor must find out for himself how it works where he resides.

In 1970 the Consumer Credit Protection Act set a limit on the amount of salary or wages that can be garnisheed: either one-quarter of the debtor's takehome pay; or the amount of weekly earnings minus thirty times the minimum hourly wage. The law also provides protection for the debtor; it now prevents an employer from discharging an employee for being in debt.

PROPER PROCEDURE FOR GARNISHMENT

In moving to intercept a debtor's income from his employer, the creditor first files an affidavit for attachment and garnishment, setting forth the facts and history of the case. The court issues an order which requires the garnishee (debtor's employer) to appear in court to answer to the amount of money owed to the debtor. Note that an entirely innocent participant in this action is brought into court. The creditor should be aware from the first of the animosity generated by this act, not only by the debtor, but by the debtor's employer as well.

If the garnishee fails to appear in court, the creditor must then proceed against the garnishee—the employer of the debtor—*in his own name!*

Eventually the money may be forthcoming to the creditor. Because of the incredible amount of activity involved in this act of obtaining money, the creditor should only turn to garnishment as a last possible resort. Many states make a garnishment process a purposely complicated one—Florida, Texas, New York, and the Carolinas are among them. Some make it easy. In general, a survey recently showed that in some large companies almost 2 percent—two employees in a hundred!—are having their wages garnisheed to pay off debts.

THE RIGHT OF A MECHANIC'S LIEN

For the individual proprietor who performs a service or provides goods for a client, the mechanic's lien can become a good weapon to use in a last-ditch effort to obtain payment for services rendered. Although all states have different kinds of statutes, all provide some kind of coverage to help the individual to force payment of overdue bills for services.

The mechanic's lien can be obtained for construction work, repair work, or alterations of a building or any kinds of improvements upon realty. One such law provides that a mechanic's lien becomes effective simply by being filed in the county recorder's office within sixty days after completion of the work. The lien does not bind the property for more than ninety days after filing, unless court proceedings are begun to enforce it. Even then, the action has to be brought to trial within two years after it is started.

A mechanic's lien, for all the complicated details involved in its execution in the various states, is a powerful weapon if properly used. Such a lien takes priority over any lien, mortgage or other encumbrance that was unrecorded at the time the work started. However, the steps in the procedure of executing such a lien vary from place to place. The individual proprietor should have a lawyer or knowledgeable agent handle the matter for him.

THE COST OF AN ATTORNEY

Attorney fees are expensive. What is more, most lawyers won't accept collection jobs unless they involve fairly substantial sums of money. It is really uneconomical to hire an attorney unless the sum is $1000 or more. With sums under $1000, the small proprietor, professional or businessperson should make use of the small claims court.

The average lawyer charges about $50 an hour for his work. One rule of thumb says that the hourly fee an attorney charges is based on twice his annual income divided by a thousand. Thus, if a lawyer earns an income of $25,000 a year, he would charge $50 for his time. All court time counts, of course, even if everyone is simply sitting around waiting for something to happen.

CHAPTER EIGHTEEN

Danger: Bankruptcy!

For the creditor, bankruptcy is the final dodge to forestall the proper settlement of an unpaid account. For the debtor it is the last resort in the attainment of relief from indebtedness. At one time in the history of the country, bankruptcy was considered a scandalous and denigrating misfortune. Today the act of bankruptcy is considered in some cases a shrewd and rewarding move for the bankrupt.

Simply put, without going into detail over the various nuances possible in its various forms, bankruptcy is the voluntary or involuntary act of a debtor to declare himself insolvent in the courts. Each creditor is then entitled to divide up whatever assets remain, convert them into cash, and receive a percentage according to the size of his claim.

For the creditor, bankruptcy has as many disadvantages as advantages. The advantage, of course, is that the creditor will get *something* out of a debt that has remained long on the books. The disadvantage is obvious: The creditor will not get the full amount of the overdue money. Statistics show that a recovery of from 10 to 15 percent of the actual amount represented by the bankruptcy claim is the average.

For the debtor, bankruptcy has the main advantage of allowing him to get out from under an intolerable financial burden and try to start up again.

WHAT THE BANKRUPTCY LAWS MEAN

Because business is generally run on credit today—extending all the way to personal credit with credit cards and charge accounts—the need for good bankruptcy laws is as great as it ever was. Credit implies risk. Even the most honest businessperson may get in over his head without committing any crime. Bankruptcy allows the honest individual debtor an opportunity to continue working in order to pay off debts that have become unbearable.

In addition to this opportunity provided for the debtor, bankruptcy allows the creditor to obtain some of the money owed him. The law treats all creditors equally, with the allotment of assets in accordance with the amount of the debts. This provision prevents the more powerful creditor from taking all the money before it is available to the small creditors.

Statistics show that only about 10 percent of businesspersons in serious debt declare bankruptcy in order to pay off their creditors. The rest continue in operation and try to pay off their debts one by one.

THE VARIOUS TYPES OF BANKRUPTCY

There are two main types of bankruptcy: voluntary and involuntary. In the voluntary type, the debtor himself *asks* to be declared bankrupt; in the involuntary type, the debtor is forced into bankruptcy by his creditor against his will.

Certain types of debtors are not allowed to petition for, nor can they be forced into, bankruptcy—railroads, municipalities, insurance companies, banking corporations and building and loan associations. Two other types of debtors may not be forced into bankruptcy, although they may petition for voluntary bankruptcy; they are wage earners and farmers.

The two main types of bankruptcy covered are Chapter X and Chapter XI. If a firm is forced into bankruptcy by its creditors, the legal code covering the procedure is Chapter X. If the firm chooses to go into bankruptcy itself, the procedure is Chapter XI.

These two types of bankruptcy involve businesses, not individuals.

HOW CHAPTER XI WORKS

Under Chapter XI, the debtor requests that his firm be allowed to remain in business, in order to earn money to pay off the company's debts. The firm remains in operation only under the supervision of a court-appointed trustee.

After a short time, the trustee makes an intensive investigation to determine whether or not the company can survive. If the trustee decides it can, the company then submits a plan of reorganization to the trustee for approval.

When the plan is approved, the company continues to operate. All or part of the debts are then paid, with whatever money is then available. Usually it takes several years before all the company's debts are settled.

However, there is one point the creditor in a Chapter XI bankruptcy situation should understand: all *new* debts under Chapter XI take precedence over old debts. In other words, the original creditor will not be paid off until all *new* creditors are satisfied. It is the trustee's job to approve all new purchases by the company, making sure there is sufficient money on hand to pay those bills.

Under Chapter XI old debts are not necessarily paid in full. Usually only partial payments are ever possible. By spreading these payments out over several years, the trustee lets the firm continue in business and allows it to concentrate on building up revenue. If the company fails, the court will transfer it into Chapter X.

HOW CHAPTER X WORKS

In the event the trustee suspects that the company seeking Chapter XI has little chance of survival, he will decide on Chapter X instead. In a case in which several creditors have a great deal of outstanding debts, they may put pressure on the trustee to try to salvage anything that can be saved by going immediately into Chapter X. In certain instances, the debtor himself may not want to try to continue under Chapter XI and will opt to go into Chapter X directly.

Chapter X action is usually swift and immediate. The court orders liquidation of the business. All assets are put up for sale, and the proceeds are applied against the liabilities. Off the top of that money pool go the court trustee's fees, attorney fees and court expenses. What is left is divided up among the secured creditors. *Secured* means that the money owed is backed up by goods or services; *unsecured* means that the money is owed without security. Banks are usually the most important of the secured creditors. By the time the money filters down to the unsecured creditors, there is often very little left.

If there are any assets left after the secured creditors are paid off, the remainder is divided up among the unsecured creditors. As has been stated, to receive 10 to 15 percent of a bankruptcy claim would be a success.

WHAT TO DO IF THE DEBTOR GOES BANKRUPT

Assuming a creditor has turned over his collections to a collection agency at the time a debtor goes bankrupt, he should immediately contact the collection agency and withdraw the claim. Otherwise, if the agency files the claim, it will collect a normal percentage of whatever it receives from the proceedings, and take its fees off the top, leaving little for the creditor of his original claim.

When the creditor withdraws the collection agency claim,

he then files his own. All creditors get a proof-of-claim form from the court. The creditor fills it out and returns it to the court.

After that, the creditor can do nothing but wait for the court notices that advise of the status of the bankruptcy proceedings. If all goes well, the creditor may receive a small check in the mail some months later. Checks may continue to arrive over a period of several years as various assets are sold off or cash is accumulated in some other way.

TWO KINDS OF PERSONAL BANKRUPTCY

So far, the types of bankruptcy covered involve small businesses or corporations. Two kinds of bankruptcy do not involve companies but individuals. One of them is covered by Chapter VII, and the other by Chapter XIII.

Since the passage of the Bankruptcy Reform Act of 1978, it has become relatively easy for a debtor to declare personal bankruptcy and to ask the courts for help. By filing for bankruptcy, the debtor has an immediate and life-saving advantage: During the court proceedings, the creditors must all back off and wait for the details to be worked out. Also, the debtor need only file a fee of about $60 to declare bankruptcy. Since 1979, there has been a tremendous increase in the number of these filings.

HOW CHAPTER VII WORKS

Chapter VII is voluntary bankruptcy by an individual. The debtor files for bankruptcy in the courts, and the court reviews the case, eventually deciding either for or against the debtor. If the decision is positive, the court then arranges to sell the debtor's assets, usually at public auction. From the money raised, the court pays the creditor as much as possible from the proceeds and cancels out many other remaining debts.

For the debtor, Chapter VII has several favorable advantages. Usually he is permitted to keep certain of the assets for his own survival. In some states, they include $7500 equity in his home, and up to $1200 interest in his car. Sometimes he is allowed to keep $500 worth of jewelry. In California, the head of the household is allowed to keep equity up to $45,000 in his home.

The debtor filing for bankruptcy under Chapter VII is prevented from filing for bankruptcy again for a period of six years.

HOW CHAPTER XIII WORKS

The second type of bankruptcy involving an individual is Chapter XIII, covering any person "whose principal income is derived from wages, salary or commissions." The debtor petitions for bankruptcy under Chapter XIII, stating that he is insolvent and unable to pay his debts. The petition states that the debtor desires to settle all his debts by reconsolidation or extension out of his future earnings and wages.

Included in the petition is a schedule of assets and liabilities. He pays a fee for a referee's salary, an expense fund and clerk's fees. The case goes before a judge or a referee. There is a meeting of all creditors, who are given ten days' notice to appear. The debtor is examined, witnesses are heard, the debtor submits his plan of action and deposits his fee with the referee.

If the creditor(s) and the referee accept the plan, the debtor continues to work and pays off his debts according to the schedule. In some cases, there can be an adjustment made between the amount owed and the amount paid. The portion owed is paid over to the court at intervals set out in the schedule. Out of his amount an equitable distribution is made among the creditors. Usually such a plan includes only unsecured creditors.

The rate of payment in Chapter XIII is generally higher than that in the average bankruptcy case. One report shows that in the usual Chapter XIII proceeding, about 92 percent of the debts are paid off.

THE DIFFICULTIES OF THE BANKRUPTCY ACT

For the creditor, the ease of personal bankruptcies written into law in the 1978 act has made it even more difficult to exact payment of overdue money. When the debtor is a recalcitrant, he now has the weapon of personal bankruptcy to use as a threat to the creditor.

Although many debts are paid up on a much higher percentage than debts recovered through Chapter X and Chapter XI, the debtor has a greater opportunity to resist the creditor. The creditor knows that by pushing too hard he may cause the debtor to declare bankruptcy. Such an action will then put off payment of debts for months and months.

The creditor must examine the debtor and determine whether or not the debtor is the type to use the bankruptcy laws against him, or if he will make every honest effort to pay up his debts no matter how difficult it may be.

In the long run, psychology is still the creditor's most important weapon when he is making efforts to collect overdue debts.

CHAPTER NINETEEN

It's Your Money—
Go Get It!

Timidity never pays off in the business world. For the creditor who finds it difficult to collect from an unmanageable debtor, leniency and forgiveness is *not* the answer. Toughness, tenacity and deliberation is the name of the game.

The creditor who tends to give every debtor the benefit of the doubt must reexamine his own mind, remembering that the money owed is *his*. It is not his fault the debtor has failed to live up to the bargain. But it *is* up to him to go after the debtor and collect what is rightfully his!

To accomplish this, the creditor above all must know his individual customer. He must be able to see his customer's problems in relation to the economy, in relation to his previous history, in relation to his character and in relation to his current degree of solvency.

It is important to the creditor to know his own competition as well as his customers. If he discovers one of his debtors has already paid off a competitor rather than him, he must be able to determine why his competitor got ahead of him.

DETERMINING THE CREDIT RISKS

The problem of keeping the accounts receivables up to date and the cash flow in a steady stream is primarily a matter of preliminary judgment and screening of potential debtors. It is not the development of a foolproof collection system *after* a debt has been incurred. There is no completely foolproof system of collections, although there are good systems that can correct an error in judgment that permitted an ill-deserving customer or client to have credit in the first place.

Rating the customer according to his credit profile is a tediously complex but rewarding procedure. Its main advantage is in determining in advance whether or not a prospective client or customer may become a debtor with an overdue account. In prosperous times, the creditor can thus easily obviate any chance of winding up with an unpaid debt. The simple act of refusing credit makes collections quite unnecessary.

However, during economic times that are a bit rocky and unpredictable, not every businessperson, professional or individual proprietor can afford to refuse credit. Today the average creditor must take a chance now and then on a customer who might fall into the "poor risk" category.

However, by analyzing the potential risk ahead of time, the creditor can determine very accurately at what point in the overdue process to begin his system of collection techniques.

THE BEST TYPE OF COLLECTION SYSTEM

If worse comes to worst and a customer does run up an unpaid account, the creditor is faced with the need to effect total payment of the debt as quickly and as painlessly as possible.

- *Quickly,* because the longer a debt remains unpaid on the books, the more it costs the creditor—not only in psychological malaise but in actual dollars and cents.

- *Painlessly,* because if the collection procedure causes the debtor to feel too much pain, he may become lost as a possible customer in the future.

THE QUICKER THE BETTER

The quickness with which the creditor perceives that a bill is overdue is a primary measure of the effectiveness of his eventual collection. A debt that is allowed to linger on for weeks and months without being noted is all the harder to collect. A debtor who is not reminded of an overdue bill is unlikely to pay up quickly. Slowness in notification breeds slowness in payment.

An accurate and efficient billing system is a must for the modern businessperson, professional or individual proprietor. Although various filing systems enable the creditor to keep close tabs on his debtors, the computer, especially the personal computer, provides one of the most efficient methods of keeping bills straight.

Although large corporations need large computers that cost many thousands of dollars, the small businessperson can easily—and usually effectively—utilize the personal computer, costing around $5000, or even less, to manage his business accounts. "Off the shelf" or "applications programs" are available in many different software brands for bookkeeping, accounts receivable and general-ledger accounting.

Most systems can operate effectively to isolate the overdue account on the day it is overdue, simply by calling up all accounts payable on a specified day. From that point, if an overdue account is observed, the creditor can put his collection system into operation.

THE ELEMENTS OF THE PERFECT SYSTEM

Once the collection system is activated by the perception of the overdue account, it must function with precision, imper-

sonality and efficiency. There are three most important elements
in the execution of a collection system:

- It must notify and remind the debtor of his
  indebtedness with *promptness.* Any lapse of time
  or tardiness in notification tends to destroy the
  effectiveness of the notification.

- It must then act with *regularity* until the bill is
  paid. The system that notifies, reminds and then
  falters in telling the debtor that he is still overdue
  is doomed to failure. Each reminder not answered
  must be followed by another reminder, more
  strongly worded, to convince the debtor that he
  must pay up. Any lapse in the system is inexcusable and fatal.

- The collection process must be designed from the
  beginning with a special overall *systematization
  of effort*—a step-by-step procedure that increases
  in intensity, using various psychological appeals
  at different steps.

With all these elements carefully built into the system, it
should succeed in effecting payment of the overdue account.

CHRONOLOGY OF THE SYSTEM

Timing of each separate collection effort is a most important
consideration in such a system. Not only must each step follow
in chronological order, but each step must occur at exactly the
correct moment in the larger scheme of the system. A correct
step taken at a wrong time destroys the intricacy of the system
and ruins its effectiveness.

Different situations, customers and economic conditions
dictate different time schedules. Individuals and background
conditions must be studied for the correct scheduling of various
steps in the collection procedure.

THE FOUR STAGES OF COLLECTION

There are basically four different stages in any collection effort, usually involving specific steps to be taken and procedures to follow. They are:

- *The Nudge*, generally considered the first stage
- *The Appeal*, generally considered the second stage
- *The Push*, generally considered the third stage
- *The Squeeze*, generally considered the fourth stage.

The Nudge includes two different phases, one of which is the *notification* of overdue money, and the second of which is the *reminder* of overdue money. In this stage the assumption is that the debtor has simply overlooked the debt.

The Appeal follows the nudge with harsher communications, which may simply be pressures brought on the debtor, or may lead to a request for a discussion of payment of the debt. This phase is the most extended, involving the most complex series of communication efforts.

The Push is a very short stage which involves setting up the final threat to the debtor: essentially, the communication (or communications) in this stage threatens to take the debtor to court through an attorney or through a collection agency.

The Squeeze is actually collection by legal effort, using a small claims court, a collection agency or an attorney in the regular court system.

METHODS OF COMMUNICATION DURING COLLECTIONS

The most effective method of collecting a debt is for a creditor to call on a debtor in person and bring about a dialogue leading to settlement. Such a visit is not always feasible. A telephone call may be substituted, although the debtor may be hard to reach. Even though it is third in effectiveness, the collection letter is the most viable method of communication between creditor and debtor.

The collection letter is difficult to write. First of all, the creditor must be aware of the laws of libel and slander. He must also understand the way to appeal psychologically to the debtor. In addition, he must know how to write an effective letter.

Most positive psychological appeals are based on a hope for cooperation and for fair play; they generally appeal to the pride of the debtor.

DIFFERENT TYPES OF APPEALS

THE APPEAL FOR COOPERATION

The mildest of all is the appeal for cooperation. The creditor simply tries to persuade the debtor to be considerate of other people, namely, the creditor himself. The creditor is courteous and friendly; he is only asking what is rightly due. The creditor must make an effort to keep such a letter of appeal for cooperation from sounding like a poor-mouth plea to someone with wealth. It is a temptation sometimes to use self-pity to invoke compassion. Self-pity should be avoided. The appeal for cooperation should be simple, gracious and polite.

THE APPEAL FOR FAIR PLAY

The appeal for fair play can be used when the appeal for cooperation fails to elicit money or response. The most logical method of establishing the appeal for fair play is to review all the facts in the overdue account: the number of days the bill is overdue; the amount of the bill; and any other details that need to be reviewed. The creditor then shows the debtor that he has carried out his or her part of the agreement. The next logical step, obviously, is for the debtor, being a fair and honest person also, to keep his or her promise to pay.

THE APPEAL TO PRIDE

In the event that both the appeal for cooperation and the appeal for fair play are unsuccessful, there is one other most effective type of appeal: that to pride. Pride is one of the seven deadly sins; but it can be effectively used in modern communications and business. Any businessperson has pride in his ability to carry on business, in his ability to make money, in his ability to hold his head high as a member of the community. Such an approach in a letter must never be heavy-handed; the debtor should never realize that it is his pride that is being exploited. The trick is for the creditor to phrase the letter in such a way that the debtor hears about the good things he has done—his good credit record, perhaps, or his business dealings or the respect and good reputation he enjoys in the community.

So much for positive appeals. If these are not effective, the creditor can always appeal to forces that are negative rather than positive.

Two appeals of a negative nature are self-interest and fear.

THE APPEAL TO SELF-INTEREST

The appeal to self-interest usually starts out by outlining the value of the debtor's present advantages in his dealings with the creditor. Once these plus factors are reasonably detailed, the creditor then reminds the debtor that any further delay in the payment of the overdue account may cause the debtor to lose all these advantages. It should be firmly stated that getting back in the good graces of the creditor, even after the debts are paid up, would be extremely difficult, perhaps impossible.

THE APPEAL TO FEAR

The appeal to fear is simply an extension of the appeal to self-interest. In this last-ditch effort, the creditor turns the previous collection letter completely around, listing the advantages of paying up quickly, then stressing the disadvantages in detail and as completely as possible. The appeal to fear usually concentrates on the problems involved with loss of good credit standing, loss of possessions that might be attached to pay the debts and loss of money garnisheed from salary.

And, of course, the creditor reminds the debtor that the past-due account will be reported to the credit bureau and turned over to a collection agency or attorney, or the creditor may take the debtor to court himself. All this will cost the debtor more money than he now owes.

These five key elements of appeal can be used alone or in combination. They are actually the basic psychological tools the creditor can use in trying to pry money loose from a debtor. The right appeal at the right time can almost always turn the tide and bring about a welcome payment of an unpaid bill.

It is useless for the creditor to sit back and let the debtor keep the money owed. He must make use of all the aids mentioned in this book in order to collect money rightfully his.

The creditor must *never* fall into the trap of believing that the debtor is worse off financially than he is. The assumption may be totally untrue. Even if it is true, the money is actually owed to the creditor. It is his for the taking. He is entitled to it by law—by the contract, verbal, written or implied, that he made at the beginning of the transaction.

What to do?

The creditor has but to follow the rules in this book. Then, by an analysis of the debtor's attitude, by a look at his business acumen, by a study of his psychological profile, he can determine what kind of steps to take in order to make a successful collection pitch and bring in the money.

And it's never too late to stress the obvious:

IT'S YOUR MONEY
GO OUT AND GET IT!

SELECTED BIBLIOGRAPHY

Barzman, Sol. *Everyday Credit Checking: A Practical Guide*. New York: Thomas Y. Crowell Co., 1973.

Beckman, Theodore N., and Foster, Ronald S. *Credits and Collections*. New York: McGraw-Hill Book Co., 1969.

Belden, George. *Strategies for the Harassed Bill Payer*. New York: Grosset and Dunlap, 1974.

Burton, Rulon T. *How to Get out of Debt . . . and Stay Out*. Salt Lake City: Brigham Street House, 1976.

Caplovitz, David. *Consumers in Trouble*. New York: Macmillan, 1974.

Cole, Robert H. *Consumer and Commercial Credit Management*. Homewood, Ill. Richard D. Irwin, Inc., 1980.

Davis, T. *How to Operate a Successful Collection Agency*. New York: Vantage Press, 1968.

Epstein, David G. *Debtor-Creditor Relations*. St. Paul, Minn.: West Publishing Co., 1973.

Follett, Robert. *How to Keep Score in Business*. Chicago: Follett Publishing Co., 1978.

Greenwood, Frank. *Profitable Small Business Computing*. Boston: Little, Brown and Co., 1982.

The Insider's Guide to Small Business Computers, Westboro, Mass.: Data General Corp., 1980.

Kaplan, Melvin, with Drotning, Phillip T. *How to Get Your Creditors off Your Back without Losing Your Shirt*. Chicago: Contemporary Books, Inc., 1979.

Kitzing, Donald R. *Credit & Collections for Small Business*. New York: McGraw-Hill Book Co., 1981.

Libes, Sol. *Small Computer Systems Handbook*. Rochelle Park, N.J.: Hogden Book Co., 1978.

McWilliams, Peter A. *The Personal Computer Book*. Los Angeles: Prelude Press, 1982.

————. *The Word Processing Book*. Los Angeles: Prelude Press, 1982.

Matthews, Douglas. *Sue the Bastards: The Victim's Handbook*. New York: Arbor House, 1973.

Mayer, Michael F. *What You Should Know about Libel and Slander*. New York: Arco, 1968.

Morris, James. *You Can Win in Small Claims Court: A View from the Bench*. New York: Rawson, Wade Publishers, 1981.

Morris, Richard H. *Credit and Collection Letters*. Great Neck, N.Y.: Channel Press, Inc., 1960.

Murphy, Herta A., and Peck, Charles E. *Effective Business Communications*. New York: McGraw-Hill Book Co., 1972.

Phelps, Robert H. *Libel: Rights, Risks, Responsibilities*. New York: Macmillan, 1956.

Sheff, Alexander L., and Ingalls, Edna. *How to Write Letters for All Occasions*. Garden City, N.Y.: Doubleday & Company, Inc., 1971.

Smith, Brian R. *The Small Computer in Small Business: A Guide to Selection and Use*. Brattleboro, Vt.: S. Greene Press, 1981.

Smith, Gregory White, and Naifeh, Steven. *What Every Client Needs to Know About Using a Lawyer*. New York: G. P. Putnam's Sons, 1982.

Striker, John M. *How You Can Sue without Hiring a Lawyer*. New York: Simon and Schuster, 1981.

Townsend, Carl. *How to Get Started with CP/M*. Beaverton, Ore.: Dilithium Press, 1981.

Warner, Ralph E. *Everybody's Guide to Small Claims Court*. Reading, Mass.: Addison-Wesley Publishing Co., 1980.

Wittenberg, Philip. *Dangerous Words, a Guide to the Law of Libel*. New York: Columbia University Press, 1947.

INDEX

169

171